Resurrecting Song

Through a collection of extensive interviews with choral conductors, educators, singers, and professional leaders, this book documents the choral music community's journey through crisis and change during the COVID-19 pandemic and aids in its rebuilding in a new era where COVID-19 is endemic.

When the pandemic emerged in early 2020, the impact on choral music was immediate and devastating, as the act of gathering and singing together became a source of contagion and potential severe illness or death. Weaving together a wide range of first-person accounts, this book addresses the impact of the coronavirus pandemic on choral music across contexts including community choruses, professional choirs, children and youth choirs, school choirs, and choral organizations. In their own words, we hear how the community responded to the challenges and banded together to innovate, use technology in new ways, and generate changes to practice. The book also explores how the pandemic caused many directors to realize that they needed to create a more inclusive place of belonging in their rehearsals and provides reflections on the philosophy of singing and creating a choral community.

Documenting both pandemic experiences and the lessons learned from surviving and thriving, this book showcases the resilience of choral music and helps point the way to new directions for the choral community in the wake of the pandemic.

Wendy K. Moy is Assistant Professor of Music Education and the Artistic Director of Crouse Chorale at Syracuse University, New York, USA, and the Co-Artistic Director of Chorosynthesis Singers. www.wendymoy.com

Resurrecting Song
A Pathway Forward for the Choral
Art in the Time of Pandemics

Wendy K. Moy

NEW YORK AND LONDON

Designed cover image: © Stephen Sartori

First published 2024
by Routledge
605 Third Avenue, New York, NY 10158

and by Routledge
4 Park Square, Milton Park, Abingdon, Oxon, OX14 4RN

Routledge is an imprint of the Taylor & Francis Group, an informa business

© 2024 Wendy K. Moy

The right of Wendy K. Moy to be identified as author of this work has been asserted in accordance with sections 77 and 78 of the Copyright, Designs and Patents Act 1988.

All rights reserved. No part of this book may be reprinted or reproduced or utilised in any form or by any electronic, mechanical, or other means, now known or hereafter invented, including photocopying and recording, or in any information storage or retrieval system, without permission in writing from the publishers.

Trademark notice: Product or corporate names may be trademarks or registered trademarks, and are used only for identification and explanation without intent to infringe.

Library of Congress Cataloging-in-Publication Data
Names: Moy, Wendy K., author.
Title: Resurrecting song: a pathway forward for the choral art in the time of pandemics/Wendy K. Moy.
Description: [First edition] | New York, NY: Routledge, 2024. | Includes index.
Identifiers: LCCN 2023047903 (print) | LCCN 2023047904 (ebook) | ISBN 9781032361543 (hardback) | ISBN 9781032361505 (paperback) | ISBN 9781003330486 (ebook)
Subjects: LCSH: Choral singing–United States–History–21st century. | Choral singing–Social aspects–United States. | Choral conductors–United States–Interviews. | Singers–United States–Interviews. | COVID-19 Pandemic, 2020—Social aspects.
Classification: LCC ML1511.6 .M69 2024 (print) | LCC ML1511.6 (ebook) | DDC 782.5/0905–dc23/eng/20231020
LC record available at https://lccn.loc.gov/2023047903
LC ebook record available at https://lccn.loc.gov/2023047904

ISBN: 978-1-032-36154-3 (hbk)
ISBN: 978-1-032-36150-5 (pbk)
ISBN: 978-1-003-33048-6 (ebk)

DOI: 10.4324/9781003330486

Typeset in Sabon LT Pro
by KnowledgeWorks Global Ltd.

In Memory of My Great-uncle, Peter Moy and

All Those Who Lost Their Lives to COVID-19

Contents

Interviewees	*viii*
Preface	*xi*
Acknowledgments	*xiii*
Introduction: Setting the Scene	1
1 Community Choirs: Loss and Hope	3
2 Children and Youth Choirs: Resiliency in Action	26
3 Collegiate Choirs: Reconceptualizing the Choral Rehearsal	55
4 Professional Singers: Grief and Innovation	77
5 Professional Choirs: Reimagining the Art	96
6 New Choirs: Inspired to Create	120
7 Choral Organizations: Resurrecting Song	130
Conclusion: We Sing On	160
Index	*163*

Interviewees

Hilary Apfelstadt Professor Emerita, University of Toronto; former Interim Executive Director, American Choral Directors Association

Sandra Babb Associate Professor of Choral Music Education, Oregon State University

Martín Benvenuto Artistic Director, 21V

Sarah Brailey Soprano; Director of Vocal Studies, The University of Chicago

Yvette Adam Burdick Artistic Director, Skagit Valley Chorale; former Choir Director, North Seattle College

Melanie Cometa Director of Choirs, Ledyard High School

Cory Davis Artistic Director, One Voice Chorus of Charlotte

Catherine Dehoney President & CEO, Chorus America

Dominick DiOrio Artistic Director, Mendelssohn Chorus of Philadelphia; Professor of Music, Indiana University; Past President, National Collegiate Choral Organization

Kellori R. Dower Dean of Visual and Performing Arts, Cypress College; Associate Faculty of Choral Music Education, Longy School of Music of Bard College; President, National Collegiate Choral Organization

Adam Faruqi tenor

Jason Max Ferdinand Director of Choral Activities, University of Maryland, College Park; former Director of Choral Activities, Professor of Music, Chair of the Department of Music, Oakwood University; Artistic Director, Jason Max Ferdinand Singers

Katherine FitzGibbon Artistic Director, Resonance Ensemble, Professor of Music and Director of Choral Activities, Lewis & Clark College; President-elect, National Collegiate Choral Organization

Interviewees ix

Derrick Fox Associate Dean of Graduate Studies and Creative Endeavors and Professor of Choral Conducting, Michigan State University; former Director of Choral Activities and Distinguished Associate Professor of Music, University of Nebraska-Omaha

David Fryling Director of Choral Activities, Hofstra University

Joshua Habermann former Chorus Director, Dallas Symphony Chorus; Artistic Director, Santa Fe Desert Chorale

Arreon A. Harley-Emerson CEO and Artistic Director, Elevate Vocal Arts; former Director of Music and Operations, Choir School of Delaware; President and CEO, Equity Sings

T.J. Harper Associate Professor of Music, Director of Choral Activities, Chair of the Department of Music, Loyola Marymount University

Crossley Hawn soprano

Craig Hella Johnson Artistic Director, Conspirare; Music Director, Cincinnati Vocal Arts Ensemble; Artist in Residence, Texas State University

Allen Henderson Executive Director, National Association of Teachers of Singing

Robyn Hilger Executive Director, American Choral Directors Association

Jeff Horenstein Director of Choirs, Meadowdale High School

Andrew Howell Music Director, The Chorus of Westerly

Stephen Lancaster Baritone; Associate Professor of the Practice and Head of the Graduate Voice Studio, University of Notre Dame

Brian Lynch Public Relations Manager, Barbershop Harmony Society

Jane Ramseyer Miller Artistic Director, GALA (LGBTQ) Choruses; former Artistic Director, One Voice Mixed Chorus-Minneapolis

Kate Maroney Mezzo-soprano; Voice Faculty, Mannes School of Music; Voice Instructor, Yale University

Michele Moore General Music and Choir Teacher, Irwin Elementary School

Mark Mummert Cantor, Trinity Lutheran Church of Worchester

Donald Nally Conductor, The Crossing

Charlotte Reese Director of Choirs, Edmonds-Woodway High School and College Place Middle School

Troy Robertson Director of Choirs, Tarleton State University

x *Interviewees*

Eugene Rogers Associate Professor of Music, Director of University Choirs, University of Michigan; Artistic Director, The Washington Chorus; Director, EXIGENCE

Tim Sharp former Executive Director, American Choral Directors Association

Carrie Tennant Artistic Director, Vancouver Youth Choir

Andre Thomas Emeritus Professor, Florida State University; former Visiting Professor of Conducting and Yale Camerata Interim Conductor, Yale University; Past President, American Choral Directors Association; Associate Artist, London Symphony Orchestra

James Weaver Director of Performing Arts and Sports, National Federation of State High School Associations

Beth Willer Associate Professor and Director of Choral Studies, Peabody Conservatory; Artistic Director, Lorelei Ensemble

Tracy Wong Assistant Professor of Choral Studies, Western University; former Assistant Professor, Music, McMaster University

Preface

On March 11, 2020, I received a call from my sister, a public health epidemiologist. She asked, "Are you still meeting with your ensembles? Have you read the news about the virus? You need to stop meeting now."

Three weeks prior, I was excited by the many collaborations and projects finally coming to fruition. I just returned from presenting at the California All-State Music Education Conference. That momentum continued working with the Hartford Gay Men's Chorus (HGMC) in joyful but intense preparation to sing the National Anthem at a hockey game and our first GALA Festival together. The Eastern Connecticut Symphony Chorus (ECSC) and I also spent long hours preparing the masterwork, *Belshazzar's Feast* by William Walton.[1] In addition, after much time and effort, my big passion project was coming to fruition—co-leading a consortium to commission a work by Melissa Dunphy to celebrate the 100th Anniversary of the 19th Amendment.

My sister sent me additional information, including an aerosol study, and I immediately called the HGMC and ECSC chorus leadership teams. For two weeks, we canceled rehearsals, believing, hoping, that we would know more about this virus, and we could move forward with our music. Those were intense discussions and decisions made with very little information. And what little information we had applied differently, as each group had different needs. At HGMC, they wanted to meet virtually and were intrigued by the idea of a virtual choir video, so we pivoted to online rehearsals. The ECSC was not interested in meeting online and ultimately canceled the rest of the season. My last in-person rehearsal with HGMC was on Monday, March 9, 2020. My final rehearsal with ECSC was on Wednesday, March 10. Subsequently, the Broad Stage closed, and Chorosynthesis Singers' premiere of *Amendment: Righting Our Wrongs* by Melissa Dunphy was canceled.[2] In August 2020, I started a new job at Syracuse University and conducted my new choir with masked singers standing 18 feet apart in a large chapel with medical-grade air filters.

As I write this preface, I can still feel the heaviness from all these "last" moments and the fear of spreading the virus in a choral setting. I am grateful that we can now come together and sing safely. In some ways, I became a better teacher, musician, and conductor during the pandemic because I had to distill what was most important, succinctly describe my instructions, and convey my musical inspirations for each virtual project. I was blessed with singers, students, and colleagues who gave so much of themselves and made the best of each moment. These reflections are what this book is about. I had the privilege of listening to the pandemic journeys of many incredible leaders in the choral field. I anticipated stories of grief and resiliency, but I did not expect to learn of the countless silver linings. As we face new COVID-19 strains and unknown challenges, I hope you hold fast to the growth and the extraordinary accomplishments that were conquered in a time of much fear and limitations. May it give you hope for the choral art and the greater community.

Note from Lisa Moy, public health epidemiologist: This text refers to the public health population-level terms "pandemic" and "post-pandemic" periods. We acknowledge these terms are inexact and problematic. We generally consider pandemic (2020–2021, no vaccination/treatment) and post-pandemic (widespread vaccination and access to treatment). The World Health Organization declared COVID-19 a global pandemic on March 11, 2020, and announced that COVID-19 was "no longer being a global health emergency" on May 5, 2023. We firmly acknowledge that COVID-19 is still deadly and debilitating, especially for high-risk and unvaccinated populations.

Notes

1 In collaboration with the Mystic Chorale and the Connecticut College choirs.
2 Chorosynthesis Singers, *Amendment: Righting Our Wrongs* by Melissa Dunphy [World Premiere], https://www.youtube.com/watch?v=VaJpj6gnqVc&t=176s

Acknowledgments

Thank you to my interviewees for their bravery in reliving their pandemic journeys. I learned so much from our time together. Special thanks to my sister, Lisa Moy, my on-call epidemiologist, for providing pandemic guidance and feedback on the manuscript. Thank you to Elisa Dekaney for her support and mentorship. I am grateful for the meeting that launched this book! Thanks to my family and friends, especially Bryan Nichols, for their encouragement and feedback on the manuscript. Thank you to the Syracuse University College of Visual and Performing Arts Faculty Enrichment Fund for their research support.

Introduction
Setting the Scene

"Choral singing is a significant part of American life, with more than 54 million Americans singing today," according to The Chorus Impact study (Grunwald Associates LLC & Chorus America, 2019).[1] Choir members said that they sang in a choir for artistic expression, feelings of happiness, and social connection (Grunwald Associates LLC & Chorus America, 2019). 73% of those interviewed said that choral singing helps to combat feelings of loneliness.

COVID-19, however, brought this "significant part of American life" to a halt.[2] After more than 118,000 cases in 114 countries and 4,291 deaths, the World Health Organization declared COVID-19 a pandemic on March 11, 2020.[3] Subsequently, the Trump administration announced a nationwide emergency on March 13, 2020.[4] The US choral community remembers that moment as the day singing ceased. On May 5, 2020, the choral community learned that singing was considered a "high-risk" activity, no barriers made it safe, and it would take 12–24 months to create a vaccine.[5] These moments set the scene for the following narratives on choral singing during the COVID-19 pandemic. This project aims to document this significant moment in the choral art timeline and aid the choral community in rebuilding as it emerges into a new era where COVID-19 is endemic. Specifically, the book focuses on the following questions:

- How did the choral community respond to the challenges of the COVID-19 pandemic?
- What did the choral community do or learn from its time during the COVID-19 pandemic that it would like to retain post-pandemic?

The interviewees' responses to these questions will help the choral community reflect on this pivotal moment in choral music history. How the choral art, as a whole, responds to the lessons learned during the pandemic will shape its character as it moves forward in a time without pandemic restrictions.

DOI: 10.4324/9781003330486-1

Over 40 American and Canadian choral conductors, teachers, professional singers, and choral organizations were interviewed (via Zoom and in person).[6] These interviews cover the ecosystem of the choral world: community choirs (including LGBTQIA, adult, multigenerational, religious, and symphony), children and youth choirs, collegiate choirs, professional choirs, and choral organizations. While the interviews were open-ended, there were guiding questions as prompts. The interviews were transcribed, and portions were selected that best answered the questions.

The author listened and selected quotations with the ears of a singer, conductor, educator, colleague, and researcher who also experienced the COVID-19 pandemic (see preface). There were tears, laughter, and even mentions of silver linings. While the stories are sometimes challenging to hear, the lessons learned deserve to be remembered and used as springboards for the future. As former ACDA Executive Director Tim Sharp said, "It'll be interesting, and I think important to document this. In 10 years, we'll look back and maybe see more clearly what we were up against and what we did, and hopefully, what we did better and what we lost."

Notes

1 Grunwald Associates LLC and Chorus America, *The Chorus Impact Study: Singing for a Lifetime*, https://chorusamerica.org/resource/chorus-impact-study-singing-lifetime
2 On February 11, 2020, the World Health Organization (WHO) named the disease causing the 2019 Novel Coronavirus outbreak "COVID-19," an abbreviated version of "Coronavirus Disease 2019."
3 World Health Organization, *Timeline: WHO's COVID-19 Response*, https://www.who.int/emergencies/diseases/novel-coronavirus-2019/interactive-timeline#!
4 Centers for Disease Control and Prevention, *CDC Museum COVID-19 Timeline*, https://www.cdc.gov/museum/timeline/covid19.html
5 National Association for Teachers of Singing, *A Conversation: What Do Science and Data Say About the Near Term Future of Singing*, https://www.youtube.com/watch?v=DFl3GsVzj6Q
6 February 2022 through March 2023

1 Community Choirs
Loss and Hope

Interviewees

Yvette Adam Burdick, Artistic Director, Skagit Valley Chorale
Cory Davis, Artistic Director, One Voice Chorus of Charlotte
Catherine Dehoney, President & CEO, Chorus America
Dominick DiOrio, Artistic Director, Mendelssohn Chorus of Philadelphia
Joshua Habermann, former Chorus Director, Dallas Symphony Chorus
Andrew Howell, Music Director, The Chorus of Westerly
Jane Ramseyer Miller, former Artistic Director, One Voice Mixed Chorus-Minneapolis
Mark Mummert, Cantor, Trinity Lutheran Church of Worchester
Eugene Rogers, Artistic Director, The Washington Chorus

Introduction

The first chapter of *Resurrecting Song* focuses on community choirs since a community choir, the Skagit Valley Chorale, shared their COVID-19 story that prevented more deaths and inspired the research that enabled choral singing to occur safely. According to the Chorus Impact Study (Grunwald Associates LLC & Chorus America, 2019), singers join community choirs for artistic expression, feelings of happiness, a passion for singing, and social connection. While making music is central, the aspect of community is paramount. However, COVID-19 vanquished their usual way of being together. This chapter chronicles how community choirs (including LGBTQIA, adult, multigenerational, religious, and symphony) grieved the loss of loved ones, discovered ways to maintain connections, and sustained hope during a worldwide pandemic.

DOI: 10.4324/9781003330486-2

What were your choir's plans when the COVID-19 pandemic emerged in March 2020?

Yvette Burdick: I have to touch on the fact we [Skagit Valley Chorale] had the cluster outbreak in March.[1] Our first issues were being sick and having that catastrophe happen to us and then having the media attention and the international attention ... There were a lot of people who judged us for how it happened and a lot of people who were supportive as well, thank goodness. It took a while for the choir to recover from being sick. While others in the choral community in May of 2020 were thinking, "What can we do?" the Chorale was just busy staying alive and recovering, and it took a long time.

Cory Davis: Our [One Voice Chorus of Charlotte] mainstage performance for the spring didn't happen. It was supposed to be, ironically, a Phoenix-themed concert that was featuring marginalized voices, very similar to what many groups were doing around that time. Then that got canceled like a week before as did everyone's.

Andrew Howell: We [The Chorus of Westerly] were just two weeks away from doing the *Brahms Requiem*, so we were very close to the finish line of that when everything just went into chaos and then shut down. We quickly realized that that was not going to happen.... It was going to be our 40th Summer Pops that June.... We had a lot of things percolating and going strong. We were at high membership. We were starting a whole bunch of new programs. We had some after-school programs that were hitting from January of 2020, so they had gone for a couple of months. We had a non-auditioned adult chorus that had started in January of 2020, so all of that stuff was really strong and moving, and then, of course, COVID-19 shut it all down.

Mark Mummert: The Saturday before everything shut down, I had 40 singers in our choir room [at Trinity Lutheran Church], in double chorus, getting ready to sing the *St. Matthew Passion*. Then COVID-19 hit, and we had to stop that.... We had to postpone that performance, but we paid all of our professional musicians half of what they were supposed to get for that performance on the understanding that when we do it again, they would get the other half.

Joshua Habermann: The Dallas Symphony Chorus, because of the nature of the respiratory thing and because they're volunteers, decided to postpone or cancel all choral projects. We were two weeks away from performing *The Book with Seven Seals* by Franz Schmidt when the whole thing shut down.... We made part tracks, everything to teach this thing to volunteers. We scheduled 13 rehearsals because we needed that many rehearsals to even have a chance. I give the Dallas Symphony Chorus credit. They had just about learned it. Then, the whole thing shut down.

Eugene Rogers: When I got a call once the shutdown happened, saying to me, "We're going to have to redo the entire season [of The Washington Chorus]," I actually collapsed. At that point, the executive director and I began to really talk very specifically about how we were going to keep our community engaged and stay afloat financially.... I had just been announced [as artistic director]. The follow-up was going to be an announcement about the season. We decided to have a formal town hall and basically have questions and I re-announced a new season. We decided we definitely wanted to create new content and not just recycle. We knew that we were going to have weekly rehearsals on Zoom.

What challenges did your choir have to overcome? How did your focus and plans change to meet those challenges?

Burdick: We had, of course, our own brand of disagreement within the group about what would be safe in terms of our requirements going forward, whether requiring vaccination or not. We lost people because of that. That was hard. It was a lot easier after we got past that.... I had finished out my last quarter at North Seattle College in the spring of 2020. While the Chorale was sort of recovering, I did a quarter there and taught online like everybody else was doing. I developed what I called, and I want the world to adopt this nomenclature, "session choir." We did audio-only recordings.... I did that with the College and took the resulting audio tracks and put them into essentially PowerPoint slideshows with images related to the text and with the lyrics superimposed as well.... So then in the fall, I adopted the same thing to use with the Chorale.... Considering the virtual choir thing, it was clear to me that virtually nobody in my choir wanted to appear on the video. They did not want to be seen that way. They didn't want to hassle with it. As it was, those audio recordings were really hard for my singers. Lots of people questioned their ability, thinking that they weren't good enough and they weren't worthy of being included....

We started Zoom rehearsals in September of 2020. I experimented in the first few rehearsals by encouraging other members of the Chorale to sing just like I'd done with the college choir.... It became what I call the *Adam Show*. It was virtually me for two hours for rehearsal and muting everybody else just out of desperation, out of self-preservation because not everybody was good at muting themselves.... That's what we did for essentially the preparations for a Christmas concert[2] in December of 2020. I call it a concert, but we recorded five session choir pieces. I took everybody's audio and edited it myself in Logic. I had a big learning curve, but it was good. I learned a lot and put those together and feel really proud of what I did. I had help with one of the tracks.... We did an hour-long Zoom, and I presented those five songs spaced out. We had a friend of mine who's been our MC ... I had the composer from New Zealand who came on the Zoom. I interviewed him just before I played the song. We had a bodhrán player from Texas who contributed to another track, and she came on also and we talked to her. The friend of mine who's a producer, he came on from Louisiana also.... It was a fun performance and people really enjoyed it. We got a fair amount of fundraising contributions, so that helped. We lost money anyway, of course, in that quarter. That went very well, actually, very successful.

People recorded their parts and their audio tracks at home. There was one person, and I heard his track. I emailed him and I said, "I think I'm hearing really big engines. I could swear I could hear seals barking, too." It turned out that he works for the Navy at Everett, and he was recording his part in his truck on his lunch break. And yes, there were huge ships right out there and there were seals right there....

I wanted to tell you about the practice guides because in Logic you can change vocal parts with ... a vocal transformer ... So, I would sing generally three per part, three sopranos, three alto, three tenor, three bass or more, if there was divisi. Then I'd be editing them and making sure they line up and making part predominant practice guides that we put on the website in the members area. When we were doing the session choir recordings, I then took my practice guides and conducted to them and made a video click track so they could see me. I was conducting it and they were hearing the practice guides that they were also working with.

Then in the spring of 2021, the general feeling was people did not want to do the recording so much. We just recorded two songs. I prepared 10 songs with practice guides like I had done with everything else.... In the fall of 2021 late summer, the cases had been low, and it looked like we were going to be able to get back together in person for rehearsals. Then it wasn't so good for a while, so we started in September with Zoom again. I was only moderately happy about that. We'd done all of that and people were getting tired of that a little bit. We were losing attendance just a little bit.... There was a school in Mount Vernon called Centennial Elementary. They have an outdoor play space that's covered and has walls on a couple of sides. We asked them and got permission to use that through October for our rehearsals outside and it was cold ... There was one rehearsal where it was raining so hard that I could not hear the choir briefly because the rain was so heavy on the roof. People were bundled up and they were cold, and I was cold. My hands were so cold at one point that I couldn't play the piano. I couldn't feel the keys....

I have to say the Board and I have been in communication just a lot. We've talked a lot about all the steps, and they have been really supportive.... We moved inside to a new venue because our old venue was not available.... The new venue was a big, multipurpose room with ceilings 30 feet high and two sets of double doors open all the time during rehearsal. [We sang] spaced six feet apart, vaccinated and boosted. We checked everybody and wore masks during rehearsal and ran two air purifiers also in the middle of the choir, which were homemade.... We also have two CO_2 monitors that we always run in rehearsal to measure the air quality of the carbon dioxide saturation in the room, which is an indication of the potential risk of COVID-19 being present....

We did a livestream concert in December.[3] [We] still didn't feel comfortable having an audience with us, so we did a livestream. We had those doors open just like we had before. We think it was in the high 30s in the back row of the choir.... That was cold but that also went well. We prepared nine songs and had a guest violinist. [We] had just a few things aside from straightforward SATB with piano or unaccompanied. [We] did that and it went really well. It was such a pleasure, even with the masks being able to get back together and sing together ... There was rejoicing for us all when we did that.... We found that livestreaming was something that our audience really appreciated. We had a lot of members who had friends and family across the country or in other parts of the world who had never been able to come to a concert of theirs before. So, they could finally see them performing.

Howell: I think we [The Chorus of Westerly] kept hopeful for a while. We didn't give up on everything all at once. It was this piecemeal realization that this was going to keep going and keep going. We kept thinking, "Well, all right. We'll just push it off a month or so, and then we'll see what happens here, ..." just shifting plans a little bit. And then after a while, it was, "Well, scrap everything. We'll reinvent the wheel." So, right in the beginning, we started doing basically social Zooms, which I think a lot of people started. It was breaking into that world of, "Hey, we can't be together to rehearse right now ..." For the adults, it was, "Grab a drink. We'll get together and chat and see how we're doing." A lot of it was us talking, and then a few people who would chime in with things. Ryan [Saunders, Executive Director], of course, does a lot of the talking because he's good at that. We would play our old concert recordings to keep everyone in the spirit of music-making, even though we couldn't actually do it together. People would informally sing along with things, and then that turned into an actual series of exploring new repertoire that we hadn't done. We did some of the Bach *[St.] Matthew Passion*. We did some of *Considering Matthew Shepard*. We did Fanshawe's *African Sanctus*, where I would bring them through things running on the piano and then we would listen to a recording. I would share it on the screen, and we would sing through it in whatever way people wanted to do, or just sit there and sip their beer and wine, and watch it go by, but at least it was something. So, on the adult side, we had a lot of engagement. There was no way I could just sit on Zoom. I didn't want to do it myself, from the beginning, and I had to because it was what we were doing. I needed to do something to at least be a little bit of a musical fulfillment in there....

We tested the water with that [virtual choir] right in the beginning where we did *Dona Nobis Pacem*.[4] That was minimally responded to, but enough that we were able to do a three-part round thing. It was cute and worked well. It was also the beginning of us trying to figure out the technology. The recording itself was poorly synced because we were doing it in-house. We were just trying to explore WeVideo and figure out how to make all of this work. It was a big learning curve on that, which eventually, we just outsourced, so that made it much easier once we were working on bigger projects.... Then we did one for the full chorus, adults, and kids, and that was just a Twelfth Night song that we always used to do, *Down with the Rosemary and Bays*.[5] That was another one that was professionally put together for us, but everyone, adults and kids, had to figure out how to record themselves. I think we had 80 people, so it was a lot of our membership that did it....

We were also dealing with having shut down our [concert] series and not being able to fulfill the tickets that we had sold to people, and trying to still put material out to say, "Hey, don't forget about us because not only are we not performing, but we still need all your money to keep us in existence, so we can come back afterwards." All the fundraising we had to do was still the same as ever. We saved a bit because we weren't doing orchestral performances, which is where the huge outlay of money goes, but we still have the same organization, the same building, all of the payroll. We never laid anyone off. We were able to continue through this entire process. We were very lucky in that way. We got a fair amount of government help, which I think everybody did, which was enormous to help us through that. We would have not done as well as we had if the government had not actually stepped in with all of those COVID-19 relief funds.

Habermann:	Dallas was among the most aggressive symphonies in the country. They kept going through the pandemic almost continuously, but only with the orchestra and not the choir. With the choir, I tried some Zoom rehearsals. I was at my piano teaching, and they were all singing, on mute! It felt meaningless. Then for a while, we did a whole series of sing-a-longs. We went back to all our old performances, and I said, "This week, we're reliving January 2017. It's the Verdi Requiem. Get your scores out." I played their recording, and they sang along with themselves. Then at a certain point everyone had maxed out on Zoom, and we had to find a way to get together in person. The orchestra had an extra service that they couldn't use.... They said, "We'll go play the concert and we'll invite the chorus as the audience" because, at that time, they were only allowing 100 people in the hall. They played this concert with 100 of us sitting in the hall all spread out. I had taught the *Humming Chorus* from *Turandot* over Zoom, so they played it and we sang, mouths closed and masked, from the hall. It was a moment of beauty, and as it ended we just applauded for ourselves because we were both the performers and the audience. We did online auditions, so that's something new that I learned. I was worried that people wouldn't be interested but actually a lot of people auditioned. I was worried that it would skew totally young because older people wouldn't want to deal with Zoom, but it wasn't that different from our normal demographic.
Mummert:	My title actually is cantor.... I'm responsible for the music that everybody in the congregation makes, but also I do a fair amount of teaching ... But during COVID-19, that was really important because my job was really about, "How do we hold on to this singing tradition that for Lutherans is enormous?" ... I really think, nothing about practicing in your car, hearing the sound through a car stereo with a microphone ... nothing about that feels like the choral art that we make but what that thing allowed us to do, it allowed us to meet every week. It kept the choir rehearsal on everybody's schedule weekly and they just kept the routine. When it was too cold to rehearse on the parking lot in cars, my choir insisted. We met via Zoom. We checked in with one another. I did a couple of things in a Zoom rehearsal. I don't like Zoom rehearsals at all. We did what we had to do....

I am friends with ... the people who designed it [car choir system]. The guy who designed this system lives in Marlborough, Massachusetts, so just not far away from here. I got wind that he was doing this, and very, very early on, I went over to his place, and we did it. So, six cars in their driveway, and he did the whole thing. I was absolutely convinced that that was a way forward for us. Initially, what we did with the church choir was we didn't even sing on Sunday mornings. We rehearsed on the parking lot and recorded things that we would then use in the video materials that went out on Sunday mornings.[6]

Here's the other wild thing. He gave me all the specs for the system, and we spent about $1,200 for all of the equipment. That included a sequencer and everything that we could actually plug into a laptop that we recorded everything. It was pretty sleek, I got to say.... So, it was a little bit of a trick. Almost everybody in their cars created a stand to sit over their steering wheel, and they put their music on their steering wheel. Then they held in their hand a wireless microphone that was connected to a mixer. We mixed 25 different microphones into a mixer, and then that mixer sent, via FM stereo broadcaster, that mixed sound to everybody's car. What was very good was that they could hear everyone in their car, singing.... I would be on headphones and the piano. We played the piano into the same mixer. So, it really did simulate a rehearsal run.... [I would] press the recording button on the mixer. Then I would just edit it and throw that up on our website. People could sing the central hymns of the service on Sunday along with our choir. That did a lot just for our congregation....

There were a couple of Thursday nights in January that were just too cold. I had warm mittens and all that stuff for when it was cold, but when it was just seven [degrees], I said, "Look, I'm not going to be out there in the parking lot." But, like I said, they insisted, "We're going to meet by Zoom. We meet every week." I just really didn't estimate how important that was for the group cohesion.... There were a couple of times after we had rehearsed something, even if the acoustic was going to be horrible, I asked them to get out of their cars in the summer and said, "Let's just sing it live on the lot." They really responded to that because they could see one another better. It was the right thing to do to get them physically feeling like they were with one another. It was odd how everybody being in their own car still felt very apart.

Then the other thing that was beneficial for me was that I have a humongous nave, and the choir sits in a rear back gallery that is also humongous. The minute we were able to come back inside, I was able to have six singers on Sunday morning, very, very spread apart. So even before we had congregants in person, we were livestreaming our services,[7] but I was able to have six singers in the gallery singing hymns and some choral music long before most of the congregations were able to resume that kind of activity. Partly, that is because we were able to keep rehearsing on the parking lot.... We have had cameras in our space for 15 years, and we would record Sunday worship. As soon as COVID-19 hit, we migrated very quickly to livestream with those same cameras, but we were already in the practice of having a televised thing.... We did five months of livestreaming a service with just three of us in the room: The pastor, a lay assistant, and me.

Davis: We canceled the thing [Phoenix concert]. We canceled everything else ... We tried to go to a virtual format but of course, everyone left. So, we really had like maybe 70 people when we were going. We had a lot of participation in the very first virtual thing we did, which was just one stand-alone piece. It was Andra Day's *Rise Up*,[8] which was part of that concert that was canceled. I was like, "We'll just transition this one into an online thing." I blew up two computers trying to figure out how to make a virtual choir because I barely knew what I was doing.... I tried to hold virtual rehearsals which was really futile.

The first virtual production that we made was like an hour long entirely insane ... I called it *Clueless*[9] because it was supposed to be like sort of a retro thing, and because I was clueless as to what to do. We hired a drag queen to produce little skits that were interspersed with our songs and then it was a huge deal. It's like I really went overboard but I didn't have anything else to do.... And then, of course, I started freaking out about copyright stuff. I decided to do ones that matched the algorithm on YouTube so that it could like handle all of that and a couple of others. And then I did one that was a CPDL (Choral Public Domain Library) piece by some composer. He had posted it online, and he gave us permission to do it. He was very happy with the result, so that was cool.

And then I wrote a piece. It was called *Sing as One*.[10] I basically asked them why they sang. They gave me Facebook comment responses and then I just put them into lyrics and wrote a little song. I took all of that and somehow edited it into a good kind of movie that is like ridiculous. I honestly cannot even believe that I did all of that.... I decided okay, we're not doing an hour-long one [concert]. We're doing 30 minutes because it was also just long for the audience. But when we premiered it, we did the YouTube Premiere ... We had the chat along the side and everything. But then I did a 30-minute one for Halloween that was really cool. We had people dress up like the Sanderson sisters from *Hocus Pocus* and do a lip-sync to it and that was really fun. That time, I used sort of the MIDI ... synthesizer sounds to create better backing tracks instead of just the piano. I focused more on the solos and duets so that it would be the same amount of content but less work for me. That worked pretty well. I think that one was really good. And then I did one for Christmas of 2020, as well.... Literally in that closet, I would close the thing because I would make rehearsal tracks for them, too because it's a non-auditioned chorus. We would basically be on Zoom, me playing the rehearsal track and forcing them to listen to it for an hour and everyone slowly dying inside. I had to auto-tune things and sort of just take out anything that wasn't working at all. It was quite the thing.

DiOrio: The first time I met with the [Mendelssohn] Chorus was in July because July 1 was my official start date. On July 8th, we had a meeting where I laid out the virtual season for them all. It was 2020, all on Zoom. Then, we gave them the option. We told them upfront, "Attendance isn't a thing this year. You can come or not come. Come if you want. Don't come if you're busy." Some people came for two months and then fell away for the rest of the season and joined back up when we were in person again. Others came to every single event. We had a beer choir night. We did lots of things. We did everything we could to help them feel part of the community.

My first in-person meeting with them was in May of 2021 because our third virtual choir project was this, which is now a CD, *Fetter and Air*[11] ... This is a stereo version of what was an eight-track installation in an outdoor rail park in Philadelphia, which we mounted in a weekend on May 13th, 14th, 15th. But the cool thing about this is that, with the virtual chorus projects we had done, one of them was Moses Hogan's *Hold On*.[12] Another was Melissa

Dunphy's new piece for us called *A Slice of Pie*.[13] Both of those were done in the traditional way: Click track, ears, sing, record, submit it, and then an engineer stitches it all together and mutes the ones that need to be muted in places. [Laughs] This was different because we recognized that many of the Mendelssohn Chorus singers, as volunteers, joined the chorus not to sing solos by themselves in their closets with pillows but instead wanted to be with others in sort of processing and expressing.

I said, "Okay, I'm going to write basically a musical recipe with some notes for each voice part based upon text that you will submit." I asked all the choristers to submit both a text dealing with anxiety or worry and a text dealing with hope or optimism, and then to record them speaking those texts, and then to send me those. I crafted the texts into a libretto, and I set that libretto to music. The libretto included at least one of everyone's sentences. We had 67 people who did that, so that's 134 statements. And then, I made, essentially, six short segments that they could record in whatever tempo, dynamic, ornaments that they wanted. Then I wrote out some instrumental parts as well. I wrote a piano part and then I said, "Perform these and send them to me," and that became this, *Fetter and Air*, which I worked with an engineer to basically map out over eight different speakers so that it would be a 25-minute looping installation. As you walk through the park, you would hear them singing and speaking it at different places, and it turns in the middle from anxiety toward optimism and hope. There's a big sort of linchpin moment and then it would repeat and go back. It ran for two and half-three hours, three days while we were there. The engineer and I, in July of last summer, squished it down and trimmed it, just like you did with a haircut, to make it fit into a stereo version, which is what we released on Navona Records. So that's all to say that that was when I saw them for the first time. We were outdoors, it was May 14th, which is also my birthday ... and the mask mandate had just ended, so we were all outside, taking off our masks, listening to our own words of anxiety and hope being sung and spoken by us. That was our first in-person meeting, but it wasn't a rehearsal. We weren't singing together. We were listening to the work we had done.

Finally, in September, we had a retreat where I came back and we sang the *Mozart Requiem* just because we could, to come back, in a barn, outside, with masks on. We sang all the movements of it and that was our return. And then, I held auditions, and the audition for anyone returning was, "You're in." I wasn't going to turn anyone away because that didn't feel right, so I called them "hearings." If they'd ever sung with us in person, they were welcome to come back immediately. I just wanted to hear their voice, so I knew how to place them. If they'd never sung with us in person, they had to do an actual audition. There were a few people we had to turn away, but nearly everyone who sang with us virtually also got to sing with us this year. We started rehearsals in October because we were just playing it really conservatively with regard to when we begin. We sang every rehearsal masked and we're a fully vaccinated chorus....

We have engagements with the Philadelphia Orchestra in December. We had five concerts and they had us tested at the start of the run and tested at the end. Every singer was negative both times.... This was when Omicron was starting to be crazy ... and there was another concert around our time. I think Joe Miller and Julian Wachner were preparing a Messiah and they had to replace all the soloists and Julian because they had unmasked coaching and three of them got sick. We were performing in that space the same day and our volunteer singers found out at 3:30 that they needed to have a negative test by 6:00 pm. They needed to leave work early to come to the orchestra to get the test so that they could sing the final concert that night. So, we did it as best we could, but all of them were negative. That's the thing, the masking really made a difference for us. Even now [Spring 2022], we're still masking, although we're starting to have conversations about how and when to relax that.

Rogers: Instead of our normal Christmas [program], which was our big moneymaker, we [The Washington Chorus] decided to film a concert[14] in that space, all-out highly, highly produced with as many people as they would allow. Then we planned to do three digital programs and another spring concert. In addition to the first digital program, we wanted to create something new. We had originally commissioned Damien Geter, and we were going to do his *Justice Symphony*. Then, we commissioned him to write us something specifically for our learning online that we would produce audio-wise. The *Cantata [For A More Hopeful*

Tomorrow][15] came out of us saying, "Well, since we were going to use him, let's have him do something else," because we wanted our mission to show that we were about championing BIPOC (Black, Indigenous, People Of Color) composers and women. We wanted to make sure that whatever we did, it still was connected to our mission.... We produced new content ... and it about burned people out. Our engineers were in Houston, so I made several trips to Houston and sat in their studio, creating sounds. I worked with the engineer to do what I normally would in a rehearsal: "I need more of a diminuendo here. I need these consonants to be together."

I started a new job on Zoom. I did all of my auditions with The Washington Chorus virtually. They made introductions of themselves and sang for me so that I could watch it asynchronously. For the most part, we took every person who auditioned, but all of those people had to re-audition. The rule was if you did a virtual audition, you had to do an in-person one. So, then the question was, "Do you audition the whole choir again?" COVID-19 was not the time to be cutting anybody. Our numbers stayed around 100 to 120 during COVID-19 and we decided to open our membership nationally. We had one person even from Singapore in addition to people locally.

The fall was easier to keep people engaged than the winter. People were less enthused in the winter because we didn't have a concert. After Christmas, the next concert was in June. We did an open sing, but people had a lot of time. It was hard to keep people engaged after the amount of work they had to put in in the fall to keep them coming back. Luckily, we still had it. Our numbers never went lower than 80 people.... When we came back from COVID-19, we had not suffered at all. I believe it's because of the amount of engagement.

There were some challenges for The Washington Chorus. For the first year, the issue was how to rehearse and keep people engaged and motivated to keep making these tracks over and over again. Teaching a community chorus that much new music, "Do you keep your assistant conductor?" We let them go, which was a tough thing for the year. We kept our professional singers only to lay the tracks, which was great for engaging them to create. They were the voices in our tracks and our mixes. Another challenge was making things stand out when everybody was producing virtual content and trying to do something different.

| | Our Christmas concert always collaborated with a high school, so we did a virtual project with the Duke Ellington School.[16] We did virtual Halloween parties and happy hours online. We collaborated with the Berkshire Choral Festival and did some open sings with intro sessions.

Our biggest challenge was how to keep revenue going. We added donations to the ticket sales online. We found that we got more donations because people were always willing to add 20 or 100 more dollars to their tickets because they knew we were online. To raise money and keep people engaged, my colleague created *Cause for Song*[17] where people could buy singing telegrams for Valentine's, Mother's Day, Christmas ... People loved the personal telegrams.... Then we created a *Cause for Song, a platform*, where people could hire guests through our platform. A legitimate concern was how to keep the board engaged. We did, but again, the board still now meets virtually.

Miller: My own chorus [One Voice Mixed Chorus] did fine financially because we received grants and PPP (Paycheck Protection Program) government assistance ... One Voice does a community engagement tour to Greater Minnesota almost every fall. We had a $20,000 grant to pay for a tour in fall 2020. It was going to be a concert exploring mental health and we couldn't go, obviously, so we reworked the grant to create a series of podcasts[18] exploring the experience of queer artists in greater Minnesota. We've had over 20,000 listens.... Each podcast features a piece of music that One Voice has performed.

In September 2021, we premiered a film that we produced called *Remembering: Singing Water*.[19] We worked on the film over the summer and then premiered it outdoors, so that was our first live event after COVID-19. The film explores Minnesota as a place of both homecoming and exile for LGBTQ people, for Indigenous people, and for immigrants. We worked with a puppet artist to have huge life-sized puppets that helped to tell the stories.... We received multiple grants and recorded all the music on people's phones, edited the soundtrack, and then filmed the stories and music with the chorus outside. We hired a professional film crew and in June, we went down by the Mississippi River and recorded all the visual shots.

Sharp: We've [Tulsa Chorale] performed, but we were outdoors, or we did a drive-in theater thing that I produced. One night, we did a performance in the large performing arts center in Tulsa for a Christmas concert. The auditorium seats 2,400 and 24 hours before the performance, the mayor shut down the city again. This was the surge in 2020 and so we had rented the performance for the thing. We'd sold tickets and then we had to shut it down. We performed it but the theater was completely empty. We livestreamed it and sold tickets that way.

How did you keep hope alive in your choir? What did you do to help your singers cope with not being able to sing?

Howell: I think that trying to keep people engaged in whatever they could was it. Again, that slow realization that we were in this for God knows how long, and that it was going to be a long-term thing, made it really hard for all of us, especially us in the office, as we realized all that. And myself artistically, to be like, "I don't know what to plan for." ... We were doing little video interview series with people where we were, again, tapping into the nostalgia of the organization saying like, "Here, we're going to talk about the tours that we've done in the past. We're going to talk about *Twelfth Night* over here. We're going to talk about the Morris Men, and that connection over here," and just bringing in some of our soloists to do things and just putting tons of material out on the internet that we never would have created normally. We never wanted to be a multimedia company. We have way more on the internet now than we ever did before.... We didn't plan to release things. Everything was archivally recorded, but I think the entire world has been a bit broken open. Everyone has everything out there now because it was the only way to engage, not only with your members but also with your audience, too.

Burdick: We did interesting things that were helped by Zoom rather than bemoaning the things that we couldn't do so much. For example, we were going to be doing the *Faure Requiem* in a concert. I had a study group that followed a regular Zoom rehearsal. We took each movement and went into great depth. I had a full score up. I shared my screen so they could look at it. I'd marked it up and showed patterns and relationships and instruments and themes. We got some really serious study of that piece in for a portion of the choir.

Mummert: Last year on Palm Sunday, we actually did the chorales from Bach's *St. Mark Passion* in our space, and we livestreamed it. The choir, instead of sitting in the gallery, was on the main floor, spread out, really, really spread out.... We had like 400 people watch it, so I think that kept the morale. In addition to the Sunday things going, we were able to make a masked livestream performance going. Everybody's morale through this whole thing suffered, but it didn't suffer so much that it took a whack at our choir.

How did the COVID-19 pandemic affect your programming?

Mummert: It has affected my programming a little bit ... Before COVID-19, I was scrupulously thinking about how the music can relate to the day and the readings of the day, the seasonal stuff. I have been choosing more comfort food (meatloaf and potatoes) for my choir, things that they actually love to sing, and not being so worried that it's going to fit necessarily because I think people need to sing things that are balm for them. I've thrown a few more of those things into the repertoire than I normally would do because I just see them hungry for anything that's going to bring comfort right now.

DiOrio: That whole first season with the Mendelssohn Chorus was about community, about maintaining that community, about still having experiences together that would help us to maybe even be more closely connected as singers in the Mendelssohn Chorus than we were prior. We didn't try and rehearse over Zoom. We didn't try and put together a whole virtual concert. We did a couple of virtual choir ideas, but we mostly had ways of gathering on a weekly basis on a Wednesday night to have conversations, to listen to a guest artist, to be part of a panel, to do a big sing over Zoom where everyone is muted, listening to a recording, and singing with their own score, to find ways of being with others and musicing, if you will.... One of the things I heard from some of the singers was that they knew more people in the chorus now than they did prior to the pandemic because, in some strange way, Zoom is an equidistant platform. You can see everyone at the same distance from you. I got to know them by name. I would be sure to address them by name in every Zoom call. As they would come into the Zoom call, I would say, "Hi, Heather. Hi, Katherine. Hi, Lilly," and go

Burdick:	down just to help them feel like, yeah, this is something that they need right now, connection, right? So, all of that was part of the need that I felt. The repertoire I chose this spring, I tried to find things that allowed them that opportunity to breathe. There's the Irish blessing ... I took it and I just separated out eight measure phrases. I inserted a measure between each of those places. It's a little bit discombobulated but it's made up for by the fact that they get to breathe on a regular basis, and they don't have that panicky feeling that builds up.... It's [The concert] about, this is something that I realized afterward, having experiences together, *Home and the Heartland*. Community coming together and expressing appreciation for us as a community.
Davis:	Yeah. I really think it is true [that COVID-19 has made his programming more emboldened] because it's like "Fuck it. I don't know when I'm going to have a chance to do it again or do whatever I want to do." I have thought a lot about ... "How am I getting to people who don't necessarily want to be back yet? How are we really welcoming people?" And then also, just thinking about like, "What do I want to do? Like I wrote a song. Do I want to start doing more of that?" ... Yeah, I think it's really pushed me further. I stopped being safe more so, I would say, than I was in the past because I think I get it. I tend to overthink things. So, when I'm programming, I'll be like, "Okay, it's a year away so here's what I should do" and then I overdo it and redo it and redo it. This time, it was like you have five seconds to make a program or else you can't do it. So, it's like all right, just throw everything and hope it works. Maybe I can somehow strike a balance between that in the future because I'm not sure which extreme is really the greatest.
Howell:	I'm excited to be looking at a normal year next year. We're planning to have a full regular season. Certainly, my own repertoire, thoughts, and choices are evolving. I've been spending a lot of time looking at new works to try and figure out how we can bring new things into our repertoire along with the classics. Next fall, we're going to do the Haydn *Nelson Mass for Troubled Times* with Caroline Shaw's *To the Hands*. ... I think, in a way, it has allowed us to branch out a little bit. It's made me think in different ways about music.

Is there anything you did or learned during the pandemic that you would keep post-pandemic?

Habermann: The online auditions were good. I think that's something we're going to keep because the singers could do as many takes as they liked. It could be their 60th take or their first and I won't know, which was fine with me because I just wanted to see them at their best.

Davis: I think the thing the organization learned is that you need to have a good infrastructure. You need to have things in place so that when shit happens, you don't just completely fall apart or put the entire burden on a single person, which is essentially what it really felt like. We're still, I think, digging out of all of that.... I think the other thing that we learned is that different people need different ways of interacting. This is something that we have started talking about now that we are in person, how to make space for neurodiverse people because we have some people who love virtual choir more than regular and they have been off doing every single possible virtual choir they can.... I do think it made us be a little bit more intentional about how we're being inclusive because that's part of our mission.... I think I've always been this way, but it made me even more focused on the process and the reason we're there, not as much the output because when we went to virtual, it was all about the output. There's nothing fun about it. [Laughs] Once you get to the product, "Yeah, it's cool, and it looks cute," but that's really not why I'm doing this or why a lot of people do it. Someone said, "The singing is our 'how,' but it's never been our 'why,'" and that really stuck with me because it's not, at least for this particular group. I've been trying to be a lot more lax and just have fun in rehearsal. I always was but apparently, I'm not as much as I thought I was, so I have tried to go toward that.

Mummert: What I learned the most through this COVID-19 experience is that whatever you can do to keep the regularity, that is the best thing because my choir, they're thriving right now. I didn't think about that when I started. I just did it because that was the only way we could stay together, but the long-term benefit was they never found something to replace their Thursday nights.... What I learned in COVID-19 was that what is almost as important as the art we have is the way this thing creates a community. So that when any of our

Miller:	choir members get sick, or somebody gets pregnant and has a baby, they're their support system, and that's beautiful. [I've learned] that time is so hard to carve out in a regular rehearsal. One of the things that I did last spring was put out a survey and asked people, "What were the things that we did during the pandemic that you want to bring back when we are in live rehearsals?" People really enjoyed getting to know each other in Zoom breakout rooms. Because I have a choir of 125, it's big and they got to be in random breakout groups of five or six people to engage in conversation. Now that we are back to rehearsals, I still plan conversational "breakout" time. The weeks we were rehearsing via Zoom, we did a lot of equity, engagement, and belonging conversations. As we moved into spring, we integrated 10-minute educational moments that happened in each Zoom rehearsal. We've continued that as well when we got back to live rehearsals as a way to make sure we don't lose that momentum that was started.
DiOrio:	Yeah. So, I think the expectations we hold of ourselves and of our singers, earlier, prior to the pandemic, were, at times, unreasonable. The pursuit of excellence is a great thing, but I've questioned a lot some of our attendance policies. I've questioned a lot some of our policies on illness and when you should stay home versus when you should come to rehearsal.... Again, that was something that I inherited from others, that many of us inherited, and I just question that preface now. And then, this maybe seems obvious, but I've always done plenty of new music because of the work that I do here [as leader of NOTUS at Indiana University], which is a new music choir. I've been programming music by women and by people who are not white for a decade, and yet, now, people are finally noticing that I do that. It's not that I would change anything, but one thing I have done, which seems quite simple, is that I now always put a picture of the composer in the program. A lot of people probably had no idea that Dale Trumbore was a woman if they were just attending concerts, for instance. I don't think we were doing a good job of communicating what we were doing prior to 2020. I'm thinking now, okay, we can probably be more intentional about the work that I'm doing in case it wasn't obvious to everyone. I think that's really important because students especially, but the community at large as well need to see that this work is important; they need to hear that the concert they just loved was actually written

	by half people who identify as BIPOC. That's important, and that shouldn't be obscured in any way. If there are ways I can make that clearer in the work that I do, then I should do that.
Rogers:	Certain things should always be online now, i.e., meetings. If the chorus has been rehearsing in person, why not have an online chorus town hall? Especially when you have a choir like ours where people are driving in from Delaware, which is like two hours sometimes …
	Nobody wants to sing with a click track again. However, if they aren't expensive, it's a tool for community choir members to practice at home. That's not a bad thing. We also learned how much we don't want to go backward but can if we have to. Everybody realized how much we value being in the same room, touching each other, feeling the vibrations, the sounds. That lesson is probably the same for everybody, but I don't want to go back ever again if I don't have to, but we can, but we know we can. That's huge …

Without prompting, some conductors reflected on positive moments from the pandemic:

Mummert:	When everyone was there pre-COVID-19, I had 23 and a balanced group … and absolutely could do anything. They remained very faithful through COVID-19. Because we kept singing and rehearsing in chorus during COVID-19, my church choir grew because other churches stopped doing choirs altogether in our vicinity. There were some people who learned that we were singing, and they came. We actually added four new members during COVID-19.… What I found is that when I broke the group up into just six singers, they rose to the occasion. They all got better through the process because they knew they had to carry their own, whereas they could disappear into the big thing. So, believe it or not, I would assess that they each got to be better singers through the process because they each knew they had to carry their part.
Howell:	Our non-auditioned adult chorus that began in early 2020, continued online, and grew even in that time … They had a full semester last year, and so we're continuing in that. We've got an Encore choir, which is a group of elderly adults at StoneRidge

	[Senior Living Community], which I had been running before, but now is under the umbrella of the Chorus. We've started a Threshold Choir, which is for people on the threshold of life. It's not for them to sing, but a group of singers who actually go bedside to people in hospice care and bring music to people at end of life. So, in so many ways, we've been able to wildly expand because we had time to step back from the run-run-run of getting a regular concert season ready, and really say, "Okay, what are the things that we want to do for our community? What are the things that will be most meaningful and impactful? How can we be even stronger for a wider audience and a wider membership when we come back from this?" So, I think, in that way, we were given a huge gift in a lot of that.
Burdick:	King 5 News, one of the Seattle stations just contacted us again a week or two ago and wants to do an interview on us: "How are you doing two years on?" We're ready to move on past being the infamous choir from Washington State and some media people especially haven't really wanted to let us do that.... I think we're going to do that because the conflict for us has always been to some extent, our privacy, our need to grieve and experience what we experienced on our own. On the other hand, because we shared our story and also especially because the studies that were based on our outbreak helped change the perception that aerosols were a problem. If we hadn't shared the way we did, I think it wouldn't have been nearly as helpful to the world but that came at a cost.
Catherine Dehoney:	In all that panic in the spring, the Skagit Valley Chorale were heroes in my book—and I think that may have gotten lost. If they hadn't been so transparent and really willing to work with the public health officials and the researchers, I think it would have taken a lot longer to make that aerosolization link. I think they saved lives. I really do. They didn't hesitate a minute even though they were facing all sorts of bad comments on Facebook and other media about being "murderers": "How could you have done this? That was so irresponsible." But the Chorale had the best information available at the time when they had that rehearsal.

Notes

1. Los Angeles Times, *A choir decided to go ahead with rehearsal. Now dozens of members have COVID-19 and two are dead*, https://www.latimes.com/world-nation/story/2020-03-29/coronavirus-choir-outbreak
2. Skagit Valley Chorale, Heralding *Christmas 2020 Online Concert*, https://youtu.be/LLOFT8YN0g4
3. Skagit Valley Chorale, *Heralding Christmas 2021 Livestream*, https://youtu.be/QmeJJL9Ll9s
4. The Chorus of Westerly, *Dona Nobis Pacem*, https://youtu.be/aIwaNu3H8bw
5. The Chorus of Westerly, *Twelve Days Festival*, https://youtu.be/4SzUap37xW8?si=PZXE-5lz5ILA4XF0
6. Telegram, *Driven to Sing*, https://www.telegram.com/story/news/local/southwest/2020/10/17/worcesters-trinity-lutheran-choir-rehearses-inside-cars-at-church-lot/114429656/
7. Trinity Lutheran Church of Worchester, *Sunday Worship Livestream*, https://vimeo.com/trinityworcester
8. One Voice of Charlotte, *Rise Up*, https://youtu.be/RdHbThJz-cg
9. One Voice of Charlotte, *Clueless*, https://youtu.be/nhoGTOsV4Go
10. One Voice of Charlotte, *Sing As One*, https://youtu.be/h1xz7OD3l24
11. Mendelssohn Choir of Philadelphia, *Fetter and Air*, https://music.youtube.com/watch?v=IIdcb8Ee6-E
12. Mendelssohn Choir of Philadelphia, *Hold On*, https://youtu.be/Ltsr8UEOXgw?si=vWksdpK6b_5EX4Gw
13. Mendelssohn Choir of Philadelphia, *A Slice of Pie*, https://youtu.be/wU7MR7KWbb8?si=sBBgp7Sd1L8ifOFm
14. The Washington Chorus, *The First Noel*, https://youtu.be/yeVJywKQvtc?si=94MFXFHyLVA5eYr4
15. The Washington Chorus, *Cantata for a More Hopeful Tomorrow*, https://youtu.be/or4-RURCh1k?si=TdJykdZna8PisElR
16. The Washington Chorus & Duke Ellington School of the Arts Concert Choir, *Mary Had a Baby*, https://youtu.be/mn2VWzobS9I
17. The Washington Chorus, *Cause for Song*, https://thewashingtonchorus.org/experience-blog/every-occasion-is-a-cause-for-song
18. One Voice Mixed Chorus, *Sound Mind Podcast*, https://www.onevoicemn.org/performances/sound-mind/
19. One Voice Mixed Chorus, *Remembering: Singing Water*, https://www.onevoicemn.org/Remembering

2 Children and Youth Choirs
Resiliency in Action

Interviewees

Melanie Cometa, Director of Choirs, Ledyard High School
Arreon A. Harley-Emerson, former Director of Music and Operations, Choir School of Delaware
Andrew Howell, Music Director, The Chorus of Westerly
Jeff Horenstein, Director of Choirs, Meadowdale High School
Michele Moore, General Music and Choir Teacher, Irwin Elementary School
Charlotte Reese, Director of Choirs, Edmonds-Woodway High School and College Place Middle School
Carrie Tennant, Artistic Director, Vancouver Youth Choir

Introduction

Dedicated and tireless, children and youth choir directors invest countless hours to make their classrooms and rehearsal rooms a special place of learning, music-making, and community. They attend conferences and workshops in their spare time to learn about best practices and repertoire selection. They also wear many hats as they are concerned not only with musical development but also with the socio-emotional development of their singers. When the COVID-19 pandemic emerged, schools were forced to shut down abruptly, and educators were left trying to figure out how to teach and guide students online with minimal guidance. In this chapter, we hear from choir directors and teachers who "built the plane while flying it" during COVID-19's global emergence. Armed with tenacity and a love for their students, these musical leaders created new ways of teaching and engagement to enable musical learning to occur during the lockdown.

What were your choir's plans when the COVID-19 pandemic emerged in March 2020?

Melanie Cometa: We have an annual scholarship concert that happens at the end of March. We were very close to being ready to perform that. We laugh about it now, but everyone really loved the rep on that concert and so bummed it didn't happen. My top two groups were supposed to be on tour in Philadelphia in early April. Our tour got canceled first, which was a huge bummer, but I was like, "It's okay. We'll do something else. We'll record an album. We'll whatever." Having no idea. When we went home in March, I was like, "Take your Pops music," for their concert in June. I was like, "Because we're going to be dancing when you get back. We have to be ready." I really did not know what was going to happen, not at all.

Jeff Horenstein: We [Meadowdale High School Choirs] were rolling full speed ahead. It's March with festivals and it's the busiest time. I was at the Northwest ACDA [Conference] when it came down. We all thought it was going to be two weeks, and then pretty quickly I figured out that we weren't coming back for the school year. They didn't tell us that for long. It was two weeks, then it was six weeks, and then I was like, "We're not coming back." That first couple of months it was just a mess. My kids were great because they like me, but school was just a disaster. Nobody knew how to do anything. We didn't know how to Zoom. Kids didn't know what was happening. I remember they gave us two weeks off and it was kind of radio silence, like, "We're not sure what's going on. We'll keep you posted." And then after two weeks, I sent a message to my jazz choir kids. I was kind of nervous about it, "Hey, do you guys just want to meet on Zoom and talk?" And they were, "Yes!" [Laugh]. That was kind of a nice moment. It was like, "Hey, we're all going through this together. We don't know what's going on, but here we are." I opened the Zoom and we talked for about 20 minutes. Then I was like, "Hey, I'm just gonna leave this open if you guys want to hang out and talk." I left and they were on there for three hours.

Michele Moore: I had my own challenges with trying to get him [my student teacher] through student teaching virtually, with very little preparation and training. They gave us two teacher professional development days to talk us through what to do.

Charlotte Reese: We're there on Thursday for the DeMiero [Jazz Festival] with the younger jazz choir. Rob Hyatt, the director, was called away from the director's luncheon because Washington State Governor Jay Inslee had announced they were going to start limiting large public gatherings and they had to reckon with how they were going to run the festival. They ended up holding the night concert on Friday but canceled the Friday and Saturday daytime activities. I remember standing in the lobby of the jazz festival, taking emails, texts, and calls—watching this calendar that was going to crush me, just blink out of existence. It's like one after another getting canceled, closing down.... The next day the middle school ensembles were on tour. On our way to Westgate [Elementary School], they called Kate [Labiak, band director] and said, "They're canceling all field trips." She said, "We're on the bus. We're coming now." I remember being in the gym at Westgate afterward putting stuff away and getting an email from the superintendent announcing no more field trips or after-school events. We were in this weird limbo.

   The following week, different districts were announcing they were going to [close] and ours didn't announce until that Wednesday at 8 PM. It was going to be two or three weeks, and then I remember hearing from Ryan [Hyde] that Monroe [School District] was going to close until April 24th, which was like six weeks, which we thought was wildly excessive. Then that Friday, a non-student day, we had a staff meeting in the theater, and they told us, "We don't know anything, really ... We're going to close for the two weeks up until spring break. Use the rest of your day to come up with some activities for the students to do while school is closed but you can't grade them or require them. But we're requiring you to come up with activities to share." I felt bad for the student teacher who showed up that day to start working with our band director.

I think it was the Monday of spring break when they announced, "No, we're closed for the rest of the year." I was crushed because I had taught some of those class of 2020 seniors for four to eight years and I wanted that time. What does "closed" even mean? ... We didn't even know what Zoom was. We could have Zooms if we wanted them once a week. At that point, I was like, "How do you Zoom choir?" I don't know, so I made the most amazing listening theory assignments ever that I don't know if anyone did, but they were amazing. There was no schedule. It was just this long weird blank.

Graduation was hybrid. Seniors showed up and were filmed receiving their diploma while we all watched on a YouTube livestream. I had the seniors from Mello-Aires record one of our songs that we'd done for JEN [Jazz Educators Network Conference]. They just recorded to a click track and our sound tech made us a virtual video. The end result was fine as they had already learned the song.

Carrie Tennant: We [Vancouver Youth Choir] had two season concerts left in our concert season, big shows. Three of our choirs were touring that spring. We had another tour booked in the summer. We had a bunch of collaborations with different arts organizations that were really kind of cool, all up in smoke, but everybody was the same.

Arreon Harley-Emerson: In March 2020, the whole world just shifted. The Choir School [of Delaware] had already been an organization that was far ahead of its time in its outreach. It wasn't just a choir for Black and brown children. It was like, "Children don't join The Choir School, families join the Choir School." We were already providing basic social services. We were already doing wellness visits at homes, which we continued to do throughout the pandemic. We were already providing access to our community partners for food pantries and utility support, but there was a greater demand for those services during the pandemic, so we were driving toilet paper to people's homes. It took a long time before schools got iPads and Chromebooks to people, so we had reached out to our donor base immediately and had secured those resources. We were on the phone with Comcast, getting kids connected at home for Internet who didn't have access previously. It was not different work, but it was definitely much more intense, and a new way of delivering those services, but we had already been doing that kind of critical social service work. In my opinion, music education is a critical social service, and we have been just expanding the wraparound services that we deliver along with music education.

What challenges did your choral program have to overcome? How did your focus and plans change to meet those challenges?

Moore: I did Microsoft Sway lessons and embedded videos of me teaching and other videos. It was a trial-and-error thing. I had to email hundreds of parents all day long lessons that were pushed out through a Google Slide. There was no live instruction happening at all during those four months. When we got to September, the best way to put it was we were trying to build the plane while we were flying it. We were waiting the whole summer for guidance on how to best prepare so that we could do this better in the fall, because we all felt, "This is not working. We're failing miserably in front of the parents, trying to create these engaging lessons," which we all did our best.... And my daughter, she loves school, and she was really starting to lose it with the all-day-long assignments without any interaction with an adult, other than me, who was trying to teach while I was parenting. It was a mess. To be honest with you, that was just what life was in 2020.

We were told to use Google Classroom. We did summer PD [professional development] and that was where it ended. We had no idea about the curriculum because we were chunking grades for our lesson planning because to try to keep up with the curriculum was not happening. The more we tried to get into higher concentration concepts with the kids, the less they showed up. We were told, by our administration, "Look, you're the special area teachers. Have them want to show up for you. Just create lessons where they want to come to school and do fun things with them. Get them up out of their seats. They're getting too much screen time." I tried to do a lot of movement with them, a lot of modifications but I was chunking, basically, Kindergarten, 1st grade through 2nd grade with differentiation for rhythm concepts and things. But the lessons itself, like the song repertoire or the activities, were very much the same. Then the same for [grades] three, four, and five, forget note reading and melody and EGBDF. It didn't happen. We were trying to keep them rhythm reading. I did a lot of listening lessons. I did form. I did things that just weren't possible, just recorded. I had kids use Flipgrid so they could send me back things, and so I could actually hear them and know they were doing some assignments.

Now in September at the 11th hour, we were told, "Okay, so here's your schedule. You are going to teach some classes hybrid, some virtual," because at that point, we had maybe 80% of our kids at home virtual. In the first marking period, we had only a really small population that was actually in-person. On my school schedule day, I would have a hybrid class where I would push in with my cart to the classroom teacher. I had kids watching me from home. I had to engage them while I had in-person kids. We were working on a half-day schedule all last year. The classes were 20 minutes, but I had a virtual, hybrid, hybrid, virtual [schedule]. My whole day was, in the first period, I've got to get my kids on Google Meet. In the second class, I didn't need to go into the classroom. I could just take them virtually, so I was only virtual or hybrid. Most of the second marking period into the beginning of the third, we were all virtual, because our [COVID-19] numbers went way up. So, with Thanksgiving and the winter break, they just kept us out until mid-February.

I had a fourth and fifth grade chorus that was virtual all year, so I had to teach myself how to create [virtual choirs]. I did an iMovie, basically. I had kids do Flipgrids and they sang. I almost did a variety show type thing, where I recorded our Google Meets. I tried to create virtual badges for chorus, where every week I tried to focus on concepts, "Okay, this week, we're going to talk about diction." We did a lot of exercises and warm-ups and things that dealt with diction. Some days, I focused on dynamics. I did try to tie in things in chorus that I normally wouldn't teach [such as] conducting ... Then in my concert video, I used snippets of what we learned in chorus this year. I focused on the badges and what we learned through each song. I ended with individual student performances that kids felt comfortable doing. They recorded their own videos from home and I just put it into iMovie. Then I had the kids do a recruitment [video], "Why they love chorus." I used that video for next year saying, "Next year, I want you to join chorus!" It was a little different this year, but we still had fun. We still learned and I mean, I really stretched it. I kind of put it: "What did we learn? Here's our performance and why you should join chorus next year." And that was my concert.

Working with fourth and fifth graders ... I'm not in the wealthiest district. We had Chromebooks for all the kids that the district provided but not all of my kids had the right earbuds or the right technology or the at-home equipment. But I did learn how to use, "Easy virtual choir."[1] I taught my kids, virtually, how to record a track and put it together. We actually sang in parts. We did a song and I had body percussion and parts. They sent the videos, and then I had to sync it up and then put it into iMovie. So, we did end with a "Let's sing together as a group." I had to have something collaborative, so I did try but it was so stressful.

At the elementary level, you think, "Well, okay. The kids are really tech savvy. They know how to do things," but they really don't. They know some things maybe in Roblox and maybe in Fortnight, but when it comes to recording yourself in a virtual choir platform, forget it. They really need somebody there to help them figure this out. We had our vulnerability because this was the time when our district was saying, "Show us what you're doing" and "We're going to put it on the district webpage." All of the school's virtual concerts can be seen by everybody, even though in real life, it's just for your own school's parents. And we're like, "Are you kidding me? You're making us post these videos when the kids are afraid to put their cameras on?" We were not happy about that, but it was more about the kids, though because some of the kids really just came to chorus because they needed a connection in a non-heavy academic subject area. We were doing a lot of SEL (social emotional learning) stuff, just innately, before SEL was really the push, so it was just about being together and sharing our love of music. That was my main purpose of keeping the kids coming week to week, but in a year, when I normally have 75 to 100 kids in chorus, I had 20, and then it would go down. It was really hard. Now, this year, I have to keep my kids socially distanced, and I'm on a cart. I do have a room available. It's a small room but I started this year out with 25 kids. Then, for my winter concert, the kids did amazing for that few kids. I was super proud of them, and my enrollment went up to 45. That's almost twice the size. I have tons of kids, and they're eager. They want to be there. We're socially distanced and masked and just loving life, and it's been such an emotional year. The kids are just craving the ensemble experience and singing together. It's just been amazing....

It's been the whole range of emotions the past couple of years. I've been in the fetal position on the floor like, "I don't know how to do this." The morale has been low, and I'm talking about teachers who are rock solid, experienced, and hardworking. It's just been so hard because it's such an unnatural way to try to teach our subject area. The experience is different. Everybody's had to make their adjustments. There's that lack of personal connection through a screen that you get when you're in a room together.

Reese: Unlike in the spring of 2020, in the fall we had a Zoom schedule with time for each class. The elementary schedule was horrible, because they were off and on Zoom all day long, but for secondary we essentially had three hours of Zoom in the morning. You'd have your first period, third period, and fifth period, but you'd only have it for 50 minutes. And then in the afternoon you were supposedly having office hours or small group things but of course, because I had Mello-Aires (advanced jazz choir), I was creating my own Zoom schedule.

We got Soundtrap accounts for all the kids. I picked songs that I knew I had a track for or could get sing-along tracks so I could put them in Soundtrap. Teaching on Zoom, you feel like an effervescent YouTuber just sending all your energy out into the ether. Most students don't have their cameras on. I can't hear them. They don't want to sing for each other ... Everyone's going to learn every part because no one wants to sit around on Zoom waiting for the altos to learn their part when you can't even hear them. I picked parts that were totally interchangeable. I'd clip out a chunk and I'd teach it, assuming that they were singing when I was teaching them. And then we'd assign them to get on Soundtrap and record their little parts. Maybe 30–40% of them actually did that.

For Mello-Aires, I picked these two tunes for them thinking they'd be confident enough to go and record. No such luck. A few of them did, but most just didn't. It seemed every other musical group was producing virtual projects but when I proposed that, they recoiled, "Why would we want to film ourselves singing?" Okay, so that's off my plate and budget. Since they didn't want to sing, we learned jazz history, solo techniques, and theory, which they loved.

I was observed on Zoom teaching basic jazz piano voicings. I had my iPhone face-down on my piano, so I was on one camera and my hands/piano on another. I shared a Google Doc with the students where they were each assigned to a chord in the progression and had to enter in the voicing that would lead from the chord before to the following chord. The kids enjoyed it. My principal called in her assistants to come watch and was absolutely delighted with the lesson.

Theory and piano progressed to vocal arranging. I had an arranging worksheet that Suzie [Reese] got from Jennifer [Barnes] at UNT [University of North Texas] about how to write two and three part arrangements. We worked through the process of an eight-bar phrase together and had them all write some, but it was clear that some of them were more into it than others. We divided them into two groups, five of which decided to stick with arranging. My goal and my hope was that they could write a chorus of a tune.

Just as our principal was making plans to bring some kids who needed more support back to school in small groups, the governor announced that we were all going back. She had to scramble and come up with a completely new plan. In April of 2021, we switched to hybrid where students were assigned to A group or B group if they chose to come back and C group if they were staying online. On a Monday, my A group was in the room, and groups B and C were on Zoom. Then the next day, it switched around. At the middle school, I had 30 kids in choir, but on an A day, I had four of them in the room and 28 on Zoom for two hours. You know what it's like to get middle schoolers to sing. Now try to get four of them in a room to sing with 28 kids listening. There was no way. It was horrible. On the B days, I had 10 or 12 kids in person, and they were so delighted to see each other and be together, and funny. Then they realized I'm even funnier in person, and we had a great time on B days. I felt bad because one of the A kids said, "I wish I was a B day. It sounds more fun." I said, "It is more fun, I'm sorry." ...

For my Mello-Aires, since they wanted them to perform for graduation, I got special permission to have them all in the same hybrid rotation. We sang *Desert Song* by säje with a track and the arrangements that the students had written.

One of my sophomores absolutely caught fire. He showed up having written a whole chorus of *The Nearness of You*. It's full-on four parts the whole time, which is not generally how you write a tune. I was just teaching them that skill. But then he also wrote a second chorus, a new melody that felt like a vocalese, with complete four-part backgrounds, and it was good. We had to go in and tweak some stuff, but we sang that for our spring concert. In the two years since he has written us at least eight charts and started studying jazz this fall (2023) at UNT.

We held a spring concert, which nearly no other school did. Our orchestra teacher, Brittany [Newell], managed the spacing and assigning of seating. The orchestra and choir parents were seated in the great hall with all the doors open. The band performed outside in the courtyard. The singers couldn't stand close enough to each other to be overhead miked, so we miked them individually, which was unnerving to students who hadn't done that before. We set individual mics on stands where the kids were this far away, where it would work. Eleven students performed for Bel Canto and 11 for Mello-Aires and people were delighted with how well they could hear them.

Cometa: In 2020 when it became clear that we were not, in fact, coming back in two weeks, my band colleague and I wanted to make sure that our kids were still making music, that their skills didn't get soft. We didn't really see what was coming next, but we wanted them to keep working. We put out a lot of stuff for them to explore independently, and we both emphasized the importance of being an independent musician anyway. We set them up like, "Hey, do you want to record with yourself? Here are some ways to do it. Here are some places you can get free sheet music. Here are some free apps." We did it in that, it's insane, March to June window. I think I put together six or seven virtual ensemble videos, just in that little chunk of time. One of them, we prepped for when we left.... I don't remember what my thought process was. I don't know that I had fully conceptualized that we would do a virtual choir, but we made part tracks on that last day of school.

I was like, "Well, we're home for two weeks. Maybe I'll try to put something together." ... We put out that first virtual ensemble pretty quickly, but our kids were making music before that because we set them up to do the Acapella app. Then we, as faculty, tried to be good models, so we did a couple of [virtual choir videos] of us.[2,3] We picked some tunes that people would like. We did our thing to be like, "Look, we're doing it too. It's fun." Then my select group put out our first virtual choir,[4] which was not good, but it was amazing at the time. I learned from that. Then my chamber choir did the Billy Joel one,[5] which took off. That got hundreds of thousands of views. Then I was in the virtual choir business, and we were just doing them constantly. We had recording schedules and workshops that we did with our kids in class, but mostly, I felt like we were just biding time....

Then like everyone, my colleague and I kept a good eye on the Colorado study,[6] and we went to all the Zoom PDs over the summer. What we did a little differently than some people did is we did not wait for our district to tell us what to do. We made a plan and presented it to our district, of course, based on what we had learned in all of these webinars. We decided that we would not do any in-person singing or playing until, at least, after the Holiday 2020 concert for many reasons. First, of course, for safety, but more than that, we saw the rollercoaster that the sports people were on: "Yes, we can play. No, we can't. Yes, we can. No, we can't." It was horrible, and we didn't want to do that to our kids.

So we decided to just go all in on virtual ensembles. We also knew that we were plugging a hole. We were catering more to our upperclassmen who had a lot of skills, knowing that our underclassmen would pay for this in a little while. Certainly, our more advanced ensembles were more active all of last year, but for those kids, that was the end for them. They had worked so hard, and this was their junior and senior year, and that really sucked. So, we wanted to give them as much as we could. We thought that the best investment we could make for our underclassmen was not to try to give them pandemic choir, but just to make sure our department stayed very visible so that when we came back, we could work together. Of course, we did virtual ensembles with them, but they weren't buying in or capable of doing it in the same way, so we gave them other projects. We gave them really cool stuff to do, but now we're focused on the rebuild....

We also made a commitment to use that year to empower creators. We hired clinicians and composers to work with our kids. I think we commissioned three pieces last year. We did workshops with dozens of people on the Internet. We did a virtual choral adjudication. We even produced a full-length musical. It's a feature film. We did *A Killer Party*, which is a show that was developed in quarantine by all these Broadway artists who were stuck at home. I didn't want to do a show that was made for stage, and we tried to make it work on the computer. It was, wow, damn hard. It was traumatic for all of us. It was not always fun, but we're really proud of what they accomplished. I know they like looking back on a lot of it, although it is a little painful. That wasn't the experience that they imagined, but there were times when we got a little bit of that feeling.

Sometimes we would have a filming night shoot. We did a one-hour holiday concert.[7] Our librarian, incredibly, in January 2020, built a media studio in our library ... an unused closet and painted the walls green, and got this sweet camera. I don't know what kind of insider trading she was doing, but we had this resource. They would come in one at a time so they could take their mask off, and we'd film them. Sometimes we had 15 kids in the same room, not filming together, but just waiting in the library, and it felt like a concert or a gig. It had that same excitement and vibe, and that was nice.

Horenstein: Everybody was kind of scared and didn't know what was going on, so very little musically anything happened for the rest of that school year.... We did a quick virtual choir thing of, *Come and Find the Quiet Center*,[8] which was our graduation song, just so they had something to do. It was nice. In my heart, I'm fully against all these virtual choir projects. At the same time, there was nothing else for us to do. I just tried to make them at least a little bit creative and interesting, but I got to the point where I can't even watch those [videos] that were by my friends anymore....

Thematic programming is something that I always aspire to do but I feel like I'm not very good at it. If I had a community adult choir, that's all I would do but there's so much other stuff to manage when you're teaching kids that it's hard to add that layer to your programming. But I was like, "Well, this is the time. What the heck?" You know because we can't just sing on Zoom all day like that. It sucks, and so I had to come up with other content. And then also, part of the problem of doing thematic programming is we don't do that much music. We only ever sing three or four songs at a concert, and so this remote learning was my excuse to do that. I created this overarching unit for the year around the theme of resilience. I gave them writing assignments, "Create a piece of art. It could be a painting. You could write a poem. Create anything and submit it." I gave them questions of the day, "[Think] about a time that you demonstrated resilience or someone that's inspired [you]." Then since it was Zoomed, there wasn't the expectation that I was going to do a ton of music anyway. So, we just did four songs, a couple of combined things, and made a couple of virtual choir videos that tied into the theme. I didn't want to do a livestreaming virtual choir concert, so I just created a website.[9] Actually, I enlisted my wife, who's a good designer....

Harley-Emerson: We used to have four days a week of programming. During the pandemic, we expanded that to five days of programming. They're already going to day school, and so when they were coming to us, they were exhausted and needed a break from screens or they just needed to have fun on a screen that was not structured in the same way that we had before. We did smaller chunks of rehearsal and musicianship types of things. We did a lot of oral training skills. We added a Sunday in there to just kind of spread things out. It was just a day that they didn't have anything, and that Sunday ended up being a day when we got so much done. I was able to use a lot of music learning theory (MLT) online ... I'm a big MLT person, and it was super successful online for us, and the kids found it to be comforting because it provided something for them. We did voice lessons, so we sang throughout.

Then we gradually did hybrid. Hybrid was the absolute most difficult of all of it because we were trying to deal with the sound, the microphones, who can hear from home, and someone's writing in the chat. It was very difficult to manage, but we did do that throughout the spring of 2021. All the 2021–2022 year, we were fully in person at that point, still masked. We sang every day. We rehearsed and had a voice lesson each week. Many of the kids had a piano lesson each week. We started each day with a check-in like, "How's it going? Tell us what's going on in your life." A lot less repertoire we did. We still did a full subscription series concert, like a whole series of concerts, because that's part of our revenue model, so we had to do these crazy concerts. They were shorter than our normal ones, they might be an hour, but it provided more time for us to just kind of be with one another. We had significant conversations about racial inequity, and we also started a show online called *And the Beat Goes On*.[10] I was with them and helped to provide some facilitation, but the kids just asked questions of people throughout the choral world. So, Dr. Andre Thomas was on there, and Craig Hella Johnson, and Dr. Rollo Dilworth. It was something that was just really great and special, and time-bound that we didn't intend to continue once we got back, but it was really deeply important for them to have agency. We had a lot of conversations about inclusion. We had a lot of conductors of color particularly on that series and the students chose all of the guests. It was a good time.

We set the three C's: Community, connection, and consistency. I felt very early on that community-building needed to be a focus, getting people to connect with others, so we still had one-on-one mentoring, group mentoring, times for just fun, hanging out, still homework help, tutoring, all that kind of stuff happens, and consistency. I think that's the thing that we did well; not to say others didn't do it well, but we were always online. We were going to continue to have all our rehearsals. Even on January 6th [2021] when the world was going crazy, we were still on Zoom having rehearsal. You got to be consistent, and you got to be persistent; that's what I've learned about working in these kinds of communities.

Howell: We obviously lost a fair amount [of children] that just never showed up in Zoom. They had no interest. Their families were not interested but we had a core group of kids that really kept coming back … We were doing a once-a-week Zoom thing that was probably 20 to 30 kids out of the possible 50 or 60 that we normally would have had in person. So, it was still a decent number. We sang through some of the repertoire that we had been doing. Someone would share their screen and scroll while I played the piano and sang. They sang along with me, and I gave them little options every now and then to unmute and sing a phrase themselves, so they were still engaging in that way. Then, we ended every session intentionally with getting-to-know-you games.... to keep that little fun element in it so that they could see a different side of each other since we had time to do that. We didn't have a concert to prepare.

Then we started to go outside, so that was the big step with them. Way before we got back together with the adults, we took the kids outdoors. We were at a nature preserve here in Westerly, Rhode Island that they would let us use.... We had three different groups of kids that I, John, and Kathryn Aaron worked with. We had our little musicianship session, our little repertoire session, and something else, like a game. Each one of them would see the three of us. We would do 20 minutes, 20 minutes, 20 minutes, and then rotate around. The kids just stood six feet apart, and they had little spots to stand on. So, it was this crazy—large groups of kids outdoors with masks on, so it was impossible to hear, but again, people kept showing up because it was that or nothing. It was really exciting actually to be together even when we couldn't be together. It was the only way to make it work. We did that until it was too cold and too dark. When we ran out of daylight, that was when we had to stop doing it....

We did a project that was just the kids where, as part of their online rehearsals, they worked with John Trafone to create a brand-new piece of music. They, basically, from prompts, gave us a bunch of words and phrases—how they were feeling about things, and just reflecting on the world we were living in. Then John took that, and created an actual text from it, wrote music, which we then rehearsed in our online rehearsals and created an online video. It's actually on Spotify and YouTube. It's called *The Little Things*.[11] Everyone had to figure out how to record themselves, which was quite a process. Now we have this weird little pandemic gem, [Laughs] that we'll get to keep

Tennant: forever, that most people probably just want to forget about, but it's still cute to look back on.

I continued to live in the land of optimism ... for the remainder of that season, I just kept telling myself, "It can't last that long." I told the parents that we were ready to pivot right back into rehearsals at any moment. We didn't go to mandatory online anything, because the feedback that I had from the families was, "My kids ... I have to homeschool them. Please don't give us any extra added responsibilities." So, we did a sort of optional enrichment. Every week I sent out a *Lockdown Digest,* and every week I did an optional Zoom that was social-based, like karaoke ... one week we just baked cookies together. I tried to send enrichment stuff, because I had small kids at home, so I was trying to think, "What would be helpful for parents like me?" We shared online music games, and videos that were really entertaining for families to watch together, or sometimes just videos that were interesting and long enough to allow parents to unload the dishwasher. We did that until the end of May and then we broke for the summer....

In the fall, we cut our training choirs in half timewise. They had two contacts a month, so we slashed their fees, too. One contact was in person in a parkade, masked. We were at an outdoor open-walled parking garage. That was once a month with our younger choirs. Then once a month we booked workshops with culture bearers. The choirs would work with someone in Georgia on a Georgian folk song, and then they would work with another leader on Indian classical music. We built up this repertoire of rote songs and stuff through that. Our oldest choir, the senior choir, did something similar, but every week. We met twice a month in the parkade and then we did online workshops with culture bearers. We gathered together with six other Canadian choirs from across Canada to create a collective called the Bridge Choral Collective. The seven choirs met online together once or twice a month for workshops with special guests. That was our Zoom rehearsal. We had some wonderful guests—Jacob Collier and Rajaton ... Jason Max Ferdinand came in. We cost-shared all of the fees to make it accessible for all of us. We had a budget that we divided by seven, and then we did lots of social activities online with the choirs, too. The whole collective came out of desperation ... The conductors basically had a Zoom-and-cry once a week starting in March, "What are we going to do? Nobody's coming back to our choirs." ...

When VYC met in the fall, we were actually able to produce a concert in the parkade. It was called *Time Capsule*.[12] It's actually one of the things I'm most proud of in my ENTIRE career. We had only had three rehearsals of 50 minutes each because that was the maximum you could sing. The choir was divided into two different groups. I had one choir on one level of the parkade, and then up the stairs on the next parkade level, the other group was on the next level up. In a single shot, we had our amazing videographer "MacGyver" a mic tree of eight different microphones together and a camera. We sang live and recorded it. We were trying to stream it, but ... in the cement, the reception was bad. Anyway, we decided to just film it, so we did the whole set—no stopping. During the show, the kids shared a lot of ideas and thoughts and reflections.... Then in the middle, the cameraman followed me up the stairs to the other choir, and one of my other kids carried the mic tree. To fill the dead time and space, I told bad jokes the whole time while we were walking up the stairs. Then we did the second set with the second choir. It ended up being really special. The singers ... it was interesting because they said, "That felt like an actual performance." I think it felt like a live [concert] because there were no takebacks. They had trouble remembering the audience wasn't there. We had a live YouTube premiere of the show, so everybody's at home and having this out-of-body experience watching it live. I thought it ended up being really fun. We were all in the YouTube chat, and we were all super excited. That was definitely a high point.

Then it was super downhill from there. Things shut down. We couldn't meet even in the parkade. We did a virtual concert. They all recorded the audio on Soundtrap, and then each choir brainstormed what they wanted their video concept to be. There was a video team. The kids made the videos. Some of them are hand-animated. Do you know Shireen Abu Khader? We did a piece of hers, and one of my kids hand-animated it ... It's so beautiful....

I also have a very wide demographic of singers. There were kids who were like, "We only have one computer in our house and my mom takes it to work." Or they didn't have *any* devices. There were singers who were homeschooling their younger siblings and didn't have the kind of access needed, so really making something mandatory was unfair, so we didn't do anything mandatory. We had device subsidies as well for anybody who needed it ...

How did you keep hope alive in your choir? What did you do to help your singers cope with not being able to sing?

Horenstein: We did a lot of non-musical things. I would throw up an icebreaker-type question of the day on the Zoom when they arrived. As they were arriving, I would call on them. We would start the class just kind of talking, engaging as much as possible. It was funny when our school put out a survey for all the students halfway through the year that was like, "What's going well in Zoom? What's hard?" Lots of people said, "Mr. Horenstein's questions of the day were like a big thing!" [Laugh] So clearly, they just craved that kind of connection. And so, we do that in person now, not every day but you know, especially at the beginning of the year. I'll be like, "Take two minutes. Here's your question. Find a partner, answer it, and then we'll talk about it." ...

In terms of community, our choir retreat is a big deal, so we had a Zoom choir retreat on a Friday night from five to eight. I had a former student teacher of mine who was really good at team building activities help me plan it and figure out how to do it on Zoom. We did little activities that sent them into breakout rooms, and then we pulled them back in, and we talked about it. It was trying. It was all just making it up as we went but I got baby pictures from many of them who sent them to me. We played a game. I made a slide show and [played] "try and guess who it was." ...

We did this song called *Strength of Love*[13] by one of my friends, Emily Braden. She released this cool song that was kind of timely in terms of the Black Lives Matter protests. For part of our retreat, she Zoomed in with us and answered some questions. It was really just making things up as we went along to try and create some kind of cool moments for these kids. It was really hard.

Tennant: In the early days (Spring 2020), we did a weekly song challenge for parents and kids. There was a theme, e.g., *Canadian folk* or *Disney songs*. The families submitted videos, and then we chose ones to highlight on our Instagram and Facebook. We had some great family submissions, too, where the whole family recorded a song together. People really appreciated that, just to have something to kind of focus on every week. I think the biggest feedback I got was, "Thank you for making nothing mandatory," because people just needed the space to do what they could when they could and when they wanted because everybody was kind of reeling. *Everybody* was worried about school, especially in our youngest and our oldest choirs. The oldest ones, they're worried about failing their classes because they can't function online, and everything they've lost in terms of significant rites of passage—from grad ceremonies to summer camp! And then people with younger kids were sharing, "They can't look after themselves, and they need stuff to do, and I have to work." So, I was trying to give them content that would make them smile but would ALSO occupy time.

Cometa: Before the pandemic, you could have lunch in your teacher's classroom if they let you. So, my kids, of course, were always having lunch in my office, and it was a great part of the day. So, when we all went home in March, we still had lunch every day on the computer in our own houses. So all the stuff that we normally did that wasn't actually singing, we tried to still do. We kept them on just project, after project, after project, to make sure they were working hard.... Also, I grieved with them like, "Man, I want to sing, too. This is horrible." Sometimes we just wallowed in it for a little while, and I think that was important. It was and still is a strange path to try to be this leader and hold up your kids and guide them through this and be enthusiastic about pandemic choir, and really, you're aching also. So, when do you let that in? When do you say to them, "Yeah, I am miserable also." When do you try to just like, "Okay, back up. We can't change it, so let's move forward." Where is the line? It changed every day.

Is there anything you did or learned during the pandemic that you would keep post-pandemic?

Reese: I've also let go of a lot of my, "You need to do this." In piano class, "If you're not going to do it, then you haven't done it," because last year we were not allowed to grade on participation. I'd never done Canvas before, so I had to learn and reinvent my whole grading plan. You have to do the thing to get the points. What a novel idea. Now, coming back this year 2021–2022, "As a performance class, there is value in giving you points for singing, but maybe not just for being a warm body in the room." Now that I'm Canvas-savvy, hypothetically once a week we do an in-class sing where, let's say on Tuesday, I teach a portion of a song. Thursday we're reviewing it and learning something else. Friday, I say, "Okay, for Tuesday, your recording is going to be letter A to letter B. You've learned that. We've done it together. You're going to reinforce it this weekend. Then on Tuesday, you're going to come back and record." Everyone spreads out around the room. They open up their Canvas on their Chromebooks and record audio or audio/video. We sing letter A to letter B all together at the same time because that's what choir feels like, not like a year of singing in your room by yourself. Then I review the recordings and hear that the altos do not know letter B or this measure. They're all singing the wrong note. It's just giving me my Thursday lesson plan because I'm hearing individually exactly what's going on. That's been great as far as my data to inform my instruction. That's way more specific than what I would have had before. This year (2022–2023) I discovered that it's even better for Mello-Aires to record the assigned section and then hand their recording to one of their section mates for review. They're merciless, know the part, and get immediate peer feedback. They said, "Ms. Reese, why did we ever do this the other way? We should always do it like this."

Cometa: As educators in general, and including music educators, I think we needed to take a harder look at what we were doing, and why we were doing it. "Am I doing this concert because I have a lot of music that's interesting and kids are learning from, and we have a message we want to relay? Or am I doing this concert because we've always done this concert, and I have to do it? Also, why do I have to do three pieces on this concert? Maybe I can just do the one and do it great." I think it's just given us a moment to take stock of what we're doing, why we're doing it, and is it our best practice? We all had to prioritize a little differently in the pandemic, and so I think it helped us break out of some of those routines....

There's another thing we chose to do in the pandemic, and I think we'll continue to do [it] in real life. Last year, we raised something between $5,000 and $8,000 for charities that we felt strongly about for a Martin Luther King[, Jr.] scholarship for The Trevor Project. Where we could, we used those videos to bring awareness or to raise money for other groups. So, we still do that. We're trying to be more aware of what we can do as stewards to our community through our music, and not just making music to make music. We really learned in the pandemic that it's not just fun, it's not extra. It is essential to life and happiness, and we really learned that it's a privilege to make it together.

Moore: As a teacher, prior to the pandemic, I wouldn't have said I'm the most tech savvy person ever. So out of necessity, I became very tech oriented. I don't want to go back. I don't want to rely solely on technology to do the job, but I learned a lot of valuable things. I think I'm able to use them more organically, comfortably.... I've used things like Music First, Music First Jr., Chrome Music Lab, Google Classroom, and all those kinds of things virtually with the kids to try to help them create music. There are so many more, like this easyvirtualchoir.com saved my life ...

Harley-Emerson: I always was MLT-lite. I became MLT-heavy. [Laughs] I've got a theory about Gordon's Learning Theory sequence and his oral way of teaching. I found that I was doing a lot more in the aural/oral tradition when I was online, which sounds weird, but I was. I began to see that there were a lot of connections between Music Learning Theory's kind of aural conception and what could be done on the gospel side.... I think there's more exploration that is needed there on the learning sequence in music of the Black diaspora. That was a big learning for me, because I saw in my students that they were improving so much. I think it was because, even though we were doing culturally relevant repertoire for years and years and that had been a big fingerprint of ours, we all fall into white supremacy like, "Oh my gosh. You have to read at a certain level by a certain amount of time."

Tennant: One thing I learned on Zoom is, I couldn't do all of the teaching, because I just sucked at it. Everything that I'm good at as an educator and as a conductor is not something you can do on Zoom. So, I ended up using the kids a lot for tons of stuff, like team building, question of the day, breakout room topics, or breaking down and discussing the text. I realized that that is a great thing. This year I've kept doing that, even though we're back together.... Whereas before you felt like it all should be on you, that version of responsibility, but also empowering of leadership is something that I'm continuing to use. I still use breakout rooms. That's the one request that they [had] ... Although this month we're gunning for a concert, so I haven't given them any [Laugh]. We'll give them a topic, and they go and chat for five minutes in their breakout room, which is just in the space.

Howell: It was nice to explore a lot of new ways of creating together. The project that we did with the kids, the two projects really, of creating a new piece of music, and working with a composer—that was really exciting and an interesting thing that we wouldn't have typically done otherwise. I would love to do some kind of project like that again in the future.

Horenstein: Yeah, more of a focus on the team building stuff for sure. It's always something that I've recognized was important, but it's also something I'm not very good at. Over the pandemic, I asked for a lot more people for help with that and then I continued to do that in person this year....

This was pretty awesome. [In Zoom choir,] I would say, "Let's sing measure one through eight together." I would demo it. I'd assume they were singing along on mute. Then I'd ask, "Naya, would you unmute and just sing that for us?" She would, and I was like, "Great, everybody. Did you notice how she turned that last note right here? Did you notice she put vibrato right here? Naya, would you do it again for us?" And then she would do it again, and I'd be like, "Okay, this time everybody on mute sing along exactly with Naya." It worked really well. When it came time to make my jazz choir virtual choir videos, their attention to detail was way better than it had ever been in person [Laugh] because that's all we could do together. They made this virtual choir video of *I Love Being Here With You*.[14] It's really, really good in terms of their quality of performance because we did this together in Zoom. We talked about it in the moment, like, "Hey, when we get back to being in person, we should do this because of this," and so we do. So now, in Impressions, it'll be like, "Hey Savannah, how would you sing that phrase?" She would sing it, and we're like, "All sopranos, let's all sing it with Savannah."

If we have our retreat, I'll give them solo songs to learn, and we'll sing for each other. I'll give them a recording and "Your assignment is to sing along with Mel Torme exactly. Copy all of his nuances and phrasing so you're not just learning *Route 66*." Well, that worked on Zoom pretty great because they could take it and practice on their own at home and sing along and make a little recording. I was listening to these recordings the week before I was going to play them for them and they were so good. I was like, "Oh my God. This is like the first thing that felt real." I was a mess. I was in tears. Then we all got together, and everybody listened to their recordings. They were so into it. It was the happiest they had been in months.

How did COVID-19 affect your programming?

Cometa: The music that I'm picking is not what I would normally pick for many of my ensembles. My top-level group is pretty great, but my developing groups are very developing, but the good news is they are developing. It'll take a little while, but we'll move forward. What I am finding to be a huge challenge, vocally, from a technical aspect in my upper level groups is my sopranos and altos did not get the same sort of training that they [usually] do in their first couple of years.

Horenstein: I have this year, and I probably will continue moving forward, try to pick songs they have an even easier time

	connecting with the text just because this year it was for the purposes of reconnecting with each other ... as opposed to the songs which they will eventually connect to because I will force it on them and eventually, they'll go with me. But having those songs that they just love and really enjoy singing would become even more of a priority.
Moore:	There's a lot of things that changed from a general music perspective, such as decolonizing the music classroom. I think a lot of things that I had done previously without being fully aware of those underlying issues. There were things I wouldn't have done before, but there were things I was like, "Oh, really? Oh, man. I was using that song, not realizing that it wasn't the best." I had to weed through my repertoire over the course of the two years when a lot of this stuff was coming to light in discussions and professional groups, a lot on Facebook groups. Even authenticity, we've had a lot of PD training with people about doing multicultural music. Westminster [Choir College] made me very aware of that, with the whole Critical Pedagogy stuff. It wasn't a new concept to me ... And I'm in an extremely diverse school district, so I wanted to get some feedback from parents and have some representation. It's funny because I do a lot of multicultural music. I have a lot of students from other countries. It's hard to find music of those countries to represent, but I don't want it to be the token song that's done in a way that's appropriation. I want it to be the right thing. So, it's really made me kind of rethink what I do and why I'm doing it. The whole [teaching approach] of "Who am I? Who are my students?" but there is validity in that. But in terms of changing song repertoire, I think most of my decisions, based upon the challenges of teaching through a pandemic, have been squeezing in from 40 minutes to 20 minutes. And that's going to be engaging, getting them up, getting physical because the kids were sitting and laying down a lot. I wanted to have kids bring in music that interested them and try to do more student-choice things.
Harley-Emerson:	We were already pretty aware of it [repertoire selection programming], but I will say that we became maybe more unapologetic. We were like, "Guess what? Some

of y'all are just now coming to this party, but let's show y'all how it's done." A lot of people were like, "I'm so excited to explore the *Margaret Bonds*." I was like, "This will be our third time doing *The Ballad of the Brown King* and this is how it is done." ... I don't think it's necessarily been a change in the programming, but I think that we've been able to speak about it in more explicit terms. Before, I felt like, "Oh yeah, this is good. This is wonderful. Now I'm putting the pill in the applesauce." Now I'm just like, "This is where we are. This is what we've been doing, but let's talk about why it's important." ... Even though I knew these things, I was not doing a good job teaching it. My kids were able to talk about the importance of windows and sliding glass doors and mirrors and all those things. But for them, now, they get up there and they're like, "Okay, Zanaida Robles is a Black woman composer," and talking about Black feminism in choral expression. It's really great and rewarding to be able to see that level of comfort in their own synthesis of how this collection of pieces works together.

Tennant: I do think I'm programming differently because the pandemic for all of us gave us a lot more space to think about equity in programming. I always programmed very diversely, but that was because of taste, not because of equity. It's because I loved it, and I was interested in it.... Then during COVID-19 I did have more space to just think about the structure of the organization. This new program, we're just starting the second season of it this week, is called *VYC Kindred*.[15] It's a music program specifically for newcomer and refugee youth. They study Indigenous music with Indigenous leaders, and then we have a team of Indigenous youth mentors as well.

Without prompting, some conductors reflected on positive moments from the pandemic:

Horenstein: The full year of COVID-19 would've been the best choirs I ever had. In terms of student talent and leadership, both my jazz choir and my chamber choir were just like this great group of juniors and seniors who were awesome. At first that was kind of a bummer, but there was no time to be bummed out about it. We just had to figure out how to do stuff. So, looking back on it with perspective, it's like, yes, that's one side of the coin that we missed out on what could have been this really cool opportunity. The other side of that coin is the fact that those kids were so awesome, not just musically, but just like awesome kids. That's really what kept us afloat.

Moore: That first rehearsal I had in September [2021], I was like, "Whoa!" And my kids, I recorded them, I was like, "This is the most beautiful day!" I felt it from them, too. It was such a moment that I'll never forget that we actually breathed together, even though we were masked. These kids wanted to be part of that, and it just felt so good to me to be back in person....

[In the faculty choir] I have probably about 16 teachers who are amazing. They sang with the kids. The kids loved singing with their teachers. They did two songs together, and then my chorus did one alone. So, it was nice, just bringing everybody as a community back together and the teachers needed it just as much as the kids needed it....

I really am trying to see that there's a lot of good that came out of this, too. I feel there is a renewed appreciation. Some teachers, I have to say, have had a lot of negative pushback from parents. I had the complete opposite experience. I have had more emails of gratitude thanking me.... I couldn't believe how grateful the parents were; they were really patient.

Tennant: So that space to think about those kinds of ideas, which are kind of simmering in the back, but you are just pedaling as fast as you can to survive managing your organization, and there was time to think about that as well. We re-jigged the structure of our organization, how and why singers move from level to level, staffing and who does what, and our music literacy program. All this brainstorming and change was essentially because I didn't have concerts and tours. It takes up so much of your brain, producing those events and those experiences for your singers. When that part was removed, yes, it was also filled with editing recordings and putting together virtual stuff, but there was space to think. I did appreciate that time, because it's manifested in great change and positive growth for our organization.

Harley-Emerson:	It was a great time for the Choir School, and for me, it was terrible. Being in that situation was crazy and scary, though I felt that we were given an opportunity to thrive. We were doing almost exactly the same thing, and it was finally seen as valuable work. So, I guess it's a good thing, but it's also a bad thing. It almost feels like ... the pandemic and George Floyd had to be together. We were already talking about inequities in health care before George Floyd was murdered, but had the pandemic not existed, and had we not been home, able to watch this and the news coverage of it, we would have said, "That's terrible." There would have been protests, but we would have moved on. I felt like the pandemic created the conditions for us to deal with that discomfort and to grapple with it, and to watch this and to have these conversations, and to have a tool like Zoom where we could have all these webinars and experts talk about it in a way that just we couldn't have done before. So, I think overall it was, I don't want to say it was good, but it was revelatory, and a litmus test for sure, or a watermark of where we've been and where we're going.
Cometa:	One of the best parts about teaching in Ledyard, CT is that they have this huge sense of tradition, legacy, and million years. It's really hard to break out of that moment. But this one silver lining here is that it offers us a window to try some new things and do things differently because now we have no kids who have done it the old way. We certainly have some traditions that we're going to keep, but it's offered us a path forward to maybe examine what is best for Ledyard Music in this new era....

Notes

1. Easy Virtual Choir, https://easyvirtualchoir.com
2. Ledyard High School Music Faculty, *Valerie*, https://youtu.be/rrbZFlZxmoQ
3. Ledyard High School Music Faculty, *Many the Miles*, https://youtu.be/hSZlNiSPkSg
4. Ledyard High School Select Singers, *Bumblebee*, https://youtu.be/JPNo7d3hMdc
5. Ledyard High School Chamber Choir, *And So It Goes*, https://youtu.be/cWFXEWWBGF0
6. National Federation of State High School Associations, *COVID-19 Study*, https://www.nfhs.org/articles/unprecedented-international-coalition-led-by-performing-arts-organizations-to-commission-covid-19-study/

7 Ledyard High School Choirs, *Home for the Holidays Concert*, https://youtu.be/iECiDAHD0Fw
8 Meadowdale High School Choir and Orchestra, *Come and Find the Quiet Center*, https://youtu.be/ih4QmFVOQoc
9 Meadowdale High School Choirs, *Resilience*, https://express.adobe.com/page/qKys2wPJU72Po/
10 Choir School of Delaware, *And the Beat Goes On*!, https://youtube.com/playlist?list=PL9QnpZEiD6YPcZmaDTVO1wM9gVX8WYrsN&si=bU5gDg72AfZ7tNsj
11 The Chorus of Westerly, *The Little Things*, https://youtu.be/QVdmhyua9BE
12 Vancouver Youth Choir, *Time Capsule*, https://youtu.be/y5BO0mBdD6U
13 Meadowdale High School Choirs featuring Emily Braden, *Strength of Love*, https://youtu.be/aYtFfq_wVa8
14 Meadowdale High School's Impressions, *I Love Being Here with You*, https://www.youtube.com/watch?v=6vEteHIIQOc&ab_channel=MeadowdaleMusic
15 Vancouver Youth Choir, *YVC Kindred*, https://vancouveryouthchoir.com/choirs/vyckindred/

3 Collegiate Choirs
Reconceptualizing the Choral Rehearsal

Interviewees

Sandra Babb, Associate Professor of Choral Music Education, Oregon State University

Kellori R. Dower, Dean of Visual and Performing Arts, Cypress College; Associate Faculty of Choral Music Education, Longy School of Music of Bard College

Jason Max Ferdinand, Director of Choral Activities, University of Maryland, College Park; former Director of Choral Activities, Professor of Music, Chair of the Department of Music, Oakwood University

Derrick Fox, Associate Dean of Graduate Studies and Creative Endeavors and Professor of Choral Conducting, Michigan State University; former Director of Choral Activities and Distinguished Associate Professor of Music, University of Nebraska-Omaha

David Fryling, Director of Choral Activities, Hofstra University

T. J. Harper, Associate Professor of Music, Director of Choral Activities, Chair of the Department of Music, Loyola Marymount University

Troy Robertson, Director of Choirs, Tarleton State University

Eugene Rogers, Associate Professor of Music, Director of University Choirs, University of Michigan

Andre Thomas, Emeritus Professor, Florida State University; former Visiting Professor of Conducting and Yale Camerata Interim Conductor, Yale University

Beth Willer, Associate Professor and Director of Choral Studies, Peabody Conservatory

Tracy Wong, Assistant Professor of Choral Studies, Western University; former Assistant Professor, Music, McMaster University

Introduction

Collegiate choral programs are tight-knit communities of singers bound together through their shared love of singing. The singers spend hours together developing their voices, creating beauty, and deepening their musicianship. On tour, they are university ambassadors through song, connecting with the greater community. Most choral programs serve non-majors and majors, and some involve the community through town-and-gown ensembles. Colleges and universities were nearing their annual spring breaks when COVID-19 was declared a national emergency. Directors told their singers to take their music home during their extended spring break while the curve flattened over the next two weeks. Universities scrambled to make Zoom an integral feature of their technological platforms, and online learning occurred for the rest of the academic year. For the fall, collegiate choral directors researched ways to return to choral singing safely and sought methods for students to complete work and degrees. These interviews illuminate the various ways these directors reconceptualized the choral rehearsal through online classes, virtual choirs, recording projects, and JackTrip.

What were your choir program's plans when the COVID-19 pandemic emerged in March 2020?

Tracy Wong: The concert was on March 13 because that's Friday the 13th and that's how I remember it. I got a text from my [McMaster University] student saying, "Are we gonna have a spring concert? Are we having choir today?" I said, "Actually, you know what? Everything seems to be shutting down. We are not having choir but come hang at the office if you want to just sit and process." We genuinely didn't know how serious it was. I had students coming in in tears to my office and saying, "What are we gonna do if we don't have choir? What's going to happen?" It was so new for everyone and the most I could do was say, "I don't know but I'm here if you want to try and process it because I'm trying to process it too" … The choir presidents were going, "What are we telling the people? What are we going to do? We don't even have a chance to do a final sing for those who are graduating." So, I found a big auditorium in our building, and I said, "Whoever feels comfortable, you want to come and then stand apart or wear a mask or whatever you want. Let's sing a couple of songs together. Let's go live on Facebook just as a way of trying to figure this out. If we cannot say anything, maybe singing can heal it." At that time, we didn't know how bad singing was. We were like, "Let's sing to heal!" We just did a couple of practices. We went live on Facebook and said, "Here are a couple of songs. I know some of our friends are not comfortable being here. That's totally fine, sing from home." And that's how we ended our season. It was really awful but that's the most we could do because after that we had to go online.... Then the whole summer was just professional development everywhere and hopping on every single Zoom session that we could to learn how to be a technician and IT specialist.

Jason Max Ferdinand: Funny enough for us, the last Aeolians recording that has been done, we recorded it four days before things shut down. That wasn't planned or anything. We had just picked that day. It was part of the spring tour. We recorded it and went back to Huntsville. I was in school for three or four days and then we shut things down and sent everybody home.

Sandra Babb: The pandemic hit, and we were in the middle of our Northwest ACDA Conference. Our conference was actually cut short and [Oregon State University] Belle Voce was the last choir to sing at that conference on a Friday at noon. Prior to that trip, all of this stuff was coming down. Nothing had been really decided, but my dean was like, "You cannot require students to go on that [trip]." My choir at that time had 74 in it and about 14 kids whose parents said, "You are absolutely not going." They were devastated, but they didn't come. But they [Belle Voce] did sing at that conference, and that was really just like transformative for them. We had worked from being a not-so-great group over the past five years to get it to that sound and it really was awesome. But then we came back and just everything was shut down. We had planned on going to San Francisco for our recruiting tour.

Derrick Fox: We [University of Nebraska-Omaha choirs] were preparing *Seven Last Words of the Unarmed* [by Joel Thompson]. The world started going crazy and I thought, "Oh, my goodness. We really need to do this performance because we spent at least a year doing the pre-performance nonmusical work

58   *Collegiate Choirs—Reconceptualizing the Choral Rehearsal*

	and a semester learning the musical portions." We did our performance on Thursday and the school shut down on Friday.
T. J. Harper:	Going into the spring of 2020, I thought, "Okay, I'm going to kind of strike out on my own and begin to put my own stamp on things." We [Loyola Marymount University choirs] were taking an entire semester to prepare for a big spring chorale. The centerpiece was going to be Leonard Bernstein's *Chichester Psalms*, which I thought, "That's great. It's a piece we can dig our teeth into." I coupled that with Tarik O'Regan's *Dorchester Canticles* ... We were guns blazing, just so happy for everything that was happening, and it [COVID-19] just caught us off guard like it did for everyone else...
It was really awkward because the week before the actual shutdown, I went to Korea for a guest conducting clinic event. When I returned, things were kind of getting bad. When I was in Korea, they were already bad over there, but nobody knew how to shut things down internationally. When I returned, the University said, "We need you to go into self-imposed quarantine for a few days because we don't know what's happening. We don't know what this is but everything's shutting down." It was just like the world didn't exist anymore.

What challenges did your choral program have to overcome? How did your focus and plans change to meet those challenges?

Babb:	Everything just shut down. We went completely online on Zoom and people just stopped coming. They would log in for a while and then they would turn off their cameras. Then the numbers fell. I think that term people dropped out and we ended the spring of 2020 with maybe 45 ... We did all this virtual choir stuff, but kids weren't into doing those singing recording assignments. They were just so filled with anxiety and dread and all the joy was gone ... Next year, we sang outside ... after October, it just kept getting darker and colder ... But when it got below 32 degrees, I canceled class ... Everything was virtual, so the filming of the ACDA [American Choral Directors Association conference] stuff[1] was all outside. I could not have everybody in the film at the same time, so, if you look at the choir, there

are two sets of 25–30 people ... We took the masks off outside. They were all spaced really far apart, and they sang along to their recordings. Every voice was digitally mastered into that recording ... I told my colleague, Steve Zielke, the Director of Choral Studies, "I want to do this." He goes "Absolutely, we're going to pay our media production people to do all of this stuff." It was about a $23,000 price tag, which is cheaper than paying for their transportation to Dallas [for the ACDA Conference].

Fox: School shut down, and then we had to go online, like everyone. For the last concert of the semester, I programmed all premieres ... After the campus shut down, my thoughts shifted to figuring out how to just survive and my students were not into virtual choir. We tried to do one optional virtual choir project.[2] We had very low participation because they just weren't interested and never became interested in doing one during the pandemic ... Of course, we did a lot of team building activities like the rest of the choral world ... I took a collection of songs from assisted living facilities ... Then I brought the list back to the students in the choirs and I said, "Pick a song that you like from that list, and then you can perform it in whatever style you want to." I collected all of the performances and created five one-hour song compilations ... I sent those back out to the assisted living homes because at that time, those homes were all locked down. Their families couldn't see them, so this was a way for them to stay connected through music ... and it was awesome because I learned a lot about my students' home music-making ... We could talk to each other about the performances, and it helped us feel like connected within our choir community.

Harper: We were completely online. Nobody still had a clue as to how to really use Zoom for these classes. The first thing most people were doing when you'd get on there was trying to remind people either to have cameras on or off. Then, there was a whole controversy about access and Wi-Fi and kids who have versus kids who don't have. The unfortunate kids who go to McDonald's to get on their Wi-Fi, can you require them to have their cameras on? What if they have nine people in the background? So, there was that conversation. I remember breakout rooms became a big thing and then I found out pretty quickly that breakout rooms weren't accomplishing anything. Kids were going in to breakout rooms and just kind of looking at each other or going on their phones. Again, compounded by the fact that not only were we not in person but also all the little band-aids that we were trying to put in place. Not only were we ill-equipped but the students were also ill-equipped to engage in that way. Teaching and learning took an absolute dive going from like 100 to zero because there was no such thing as online pedagogy at that time....

That summer was high stress. We were all scrambling, trying to become tech experts, trying to find a million different ways, games, and strategies to engage people. For our singers who can't read music, that turned out to be really challenging. For the singers who are working at a high level in terms of their vocal technique and the number of years in the program, we were never able to meet that level for the students ... But what we did when we came back in fall 2020 was Zoom choir and we came up with a list of not just protocols but etiquette surrounding what it means to be part of the LMU Choirs via Zoom ... So, we limped along, and I was lucky. I was able to go back onto campus with my accompanist and we were able to be in our rehearsal room. And so, what we did is we broadcast from the rehearsal room. He had his camera on himself as part of the Zoom class. I had the main camera on me and then we projected on the main screen everybody. If you're looking at me, you would then see all the faces behind me. So, you still get a sense that we're all there together ... They were muted, of course. They could raise their hand if they had questions. We would take bio breaks so they can get away from the screen and not stare at the screen for too long. In a two-hour rehearsal, we would take three breaks, so we'd only be on there for about 20 minutes at a time. I was waving my arms, sometimes demonstrating and then I would stop and say, "Wow, that was really good. I can tell just by your posture that you're breathing well. Look over there, Angie has her mouth forming the perfect vowel. There's a nice 'O' vowel. Let's all make that 'O' vowel like Angie. If you're doing that, I can tell the sound is going to be really good." I was basically just cheerleading for that entire semester....

The fall semester, we had eight songs per choir, and we were going to do four virtual choir projects. We were going to practice and rehearse eight songs and then pick four that we really liked to do virtual choir projects in the spring. So, we worked on four songs and only did two virtual choir projects because people just hated the platform. They were just so sick of it, and they tried. They were being really upbeat and trying to be very happy and it was hard. The first virtual choir project we did in the fall of 2020. I think it was maybe one of Elaine Hagenberg's songs, *You Do Not Walk Alone*[3] which is so beautiful and has all the tracks. I think Dan Forrest is actually playing the piano accompaniment for that and I thought, "This is great. It's pretty. Not too difficult."

We set the recording deadlines, "Okay, this is when we're going to record parts and you have to send them in." We did it two different ways: One producer had them do audio and video at the same time. Another producer we worked with had them do audio separately and then do a lip-sync video to themselves, which was fine. The second one worked better. But what I learned was that because they were in isolation, there was no one around them to give them guidance. They were not hearing other people to blend and balance with. They were driving themselves crazy with any little sound that they didn't like, any little vowel or consonant, and they would stop it and start over. I was getting emails like at two o'clock in the morning from people in tears saying, "I've been recording myself for 10 hours. I can't get it right. What do I do?" On average, people were spending four to five hours but there were some who were taking entire days and couldn't get one clean recording. That was hard. It was really hard....

Jump forward into the spring of 2021, I was doing research like everybody else because latency [in Zoom] was a huge issue. Anytime you tried to have more than one microphone on, it just killed it.... Because we're in a very fortunate position, we were able to invest in JackTrip. So, with the audition choir, we were able to get a JackTrip device and accompanying equipment for every single member of the choir. And for the concert choir, the large mixed non-audition group, we were able to get 20 devices, so there was representation with five devices in each section. And what that did, just kind of like some of these other technologies, it almost eliminated latency. The audio quality was really good. So, we were based out of LA. I was like the webmaster, the primary person, but people in Washington State, in Maine, in Maryland, they could still hook in and there was almost zero latency. So, in the spring semester, we could finally sync together in real time. It was bonkers ... We could hear each other in real time and each individual person could adjust levels on their own end, like our brightness, whatever it happens to be. We'd have all the altos sing or all the altos and tenors sing. We could work on parts. We could work on these kinds of things. The challenges of Zoom and technology were still there a little bit, so we actually never got a clean recording of one complete song, believe it or not, because one person's mic wasn't working or headphone or ethernet cable was frayed because of a cat, all these little things. So, even though it was this huge jump forward, we still struggled. So, I don't know. It was not great, but it was something that we were able to do and compared to what we had before, there was no question. It was like night and day.

Troy Robertson: In the fall of 2020, we [Tarleton State University] split the choirs where needed because I had a big room. Since the chamber choir had 40 singers, I couldn't fit them in one room with the appropriate spacing. We sang masked through the spring ... We took a long break from live concerts. For the fall concert, I created 12 virtual choirs. We did ten for the December concert, and then I did another ten for the following spring, so I did a total of 30 some virtual choirs with Tarleton[4] ... For the fall of 2020, our rehearsal was for the sake of the virtual choirs ... We did some online rehearsals because I also was trying to preserve my sanity. We held online rehearsals on Fridays, which enabled me to say a couple of times, "All right, you're on your own. I'm working on the concert this Friday." Knowing now what that's like, I would not have emphasized that much because it's just not satisfying. This was my theory the whole time; what really matters about choir is being in the same room together. That's what matters, and that was my intention the entire time. This is just a stopgap. Because people had called me and said, "Aren't you worried that this is going to take the place of choir?" I was like, "No, not even a little bit."...

It is hard to put yourself back there, but there were economic concerns. Whenever there are economic concerns, we think, "Oh my gosh, they may cut music!" Sure enough, it did happen. I have a couple of colleagues whose departments were cut. I was just worried music might fall victim to that because of the economics, and we can't realistically do this together. So, I thought, "Well, this is not that hard, so I'm going to try to help people figure this out"...

My friend Tesfa Wondemagegnehu and I were talking about the pandemic. We started brainstorming about Chor Amor.[5] It could be something where we could really help people ... It was something I wanted to do as a resource database situation ... It's funny because the last time I checked, which was in the summer of 2021, we had 40,000 hits from all continents except Antarctica. It was remarkable ... Probably half a dozen people put forth a lot of effort to help train teachers in the summer and into the fall. Now that resource is just there. I haven't done much with it in the last year, and

Wong: to be honest with you; I was pretty burned out. With Chor Amor, I wanted to do exactly what it did: Help people with this one moment.

So besides trying to advocate for students, I found myself in a position needing to advocate for the arts and the activity itself. I had to do all the background work I could to show what I'm going to do if we're going to be online and how it's going to stay robust and things like that ...

That was pretty tough. During that summer I made sure that I experienced doing my own recordings and singing first, so I knew how difficult it might be. And then [I focused on] whatever cheat sheet and tips and tricks I could give my students ... The choir budget from acquiring music was split into some of it acquiring music, some, of course, were CPDL ... and then the rest of the money that was for music acquisition I put into a budget to hire my friend from Singapore to edit all the recording tracks. I also had another accompanist for the choir, who is also an audio engineer ...

I think the biggest feature of Zoom for me is a breakout room. Sometimes I said, "Breakout room on your own" and then it was just me left in the main room. I'm like "Ahh, there's five minutes [for me]." It's just so much brain power. I was telling Carrie Tennant [Vancouver Youth Choir Artistic Director] that at a certain point, I realized for the one-and-a-half-hour choir rehearsal that I'm basically a show producer ... and it's live! For me, the saving grace was having a student executive team that, I'm really, really glad, who were just on top of it ... I had Co-Presidents. One would lead each choir, and that's where it really helped with communication. And then we had concert producers. They helped me with the timeline of getting things in order and seeing what the YouTube situation would be if we were to put it out there ...

The end of term project was always one video recording, which took a lot of work ... The first session in the choir was teaching them how Soundtrap worked. I brought in my friend Cherie Chai, who had to tune in to us at 5:00 am Singapore time. She said, "This is your microphone and then enter that, and this is that. If you're using this microphone, that's totally fine. If you're capturing yourself on say your phone, just tie your phone with a rubber band to a can of beans and you'll really get yourself really clear." So, it's things that I never would have thought up because in Singapore they had been doing it since the end of early 2020. They shut much earlier and had their head in the game already ... I know there were some who were very much purists and said, "I just want to sing live" but I could not, and so the rest of the session for the evening was how to take care of your voice ...

I said, "If anyone needs to use a campus rehearsal space, even though it's closed, let me see what I can do to help." And then me and the band director, we would have to advocate for this ... I had two kids who were tuning in from China, so it's a 12-hour difference. They were coming blurry eyed at 5:00 am on their side and I said, "You know what? If you don't make it, it's fine. We will keep you updated. We'll have a separate check in and that's totally okay." So, we had students who were in different time zones who were still trying to do this and with really poor internet. I tried to keep it shorter and before every rehearsal I put down by the minute the entire rehearsal schedule ...

By the second term, I was like "I think we're getting the hang of it. Can we have a few student DJs get a few pieces of music together [to play] when people come into the Zoom room?" [I asked] because it was so silent when people came in. I stared at you, and you stared at me, and everyone was stuffing their faces before choir. So, there were a few people who shared their favorite music ... Then we came up with different backgrounds for different sections ... and put their names, according to the sections for us. It's easy for attendance taking ... I usually had to run warm-ups myself because it did make the most sense with the keyboard setup. My space looked like a spaceship. I turned around the camera and I showed them and said, "This is the mess I'm working with so if you're working in a mess that's fine. [We're] all in this together." They're like "Oh, okay that's good ..."

Learning how to record on Soundtrap, people were like, "Oh, no. I don't sound good. I'm not sure." I had so many conversations with different students, one-on-one, about how they didn't feel confident with their voices in the meeting. We always established it at the top of the term (only because I've been with that

Collegiate Choirs—Reconceptualizing the Choral Rehearsal 65

university for a few years now and they know me). If there's something they're not sure of, they can talk to me directly. I said, "We will be singing, and at certain points, your mic will be on for Zoom. You are in choir because you want to improve, and so am I. You're going to hear my singing, and all its worst and best anyway, so 'Let's do it together!' We're going to do a singing tag team thing, but we're only going to do it in your own section, so only people in your own breakout room are going to hear you" ...

We did a couple of videos[6,7] and that went through to the campus, so we're able to still have community engagement. We did online professional development for the choir because it's something that we do every year ... We bring in a master's student who is doing their final year thesis and [for example] talks about mindfulness as a musician ... And we actually share that session with the Hamilton Children's Choir because it is in Hamilton city ... Being able to connect with a younger community choir helped with not only recruitment but also connection. We're just all in the same city and we needed to share resources ...

By the second term, I said, "Okay we're going to rest our voices now. Let's look at audio engineering." So, I pulled it up, and I said, "We're going to listen to group number one." Everyone was like "Oh, no!" I liked that they had different pieces, so they didn't compare [themselves] with each other. I said, "In the chat, just write down things that you are really proud of that you did together and a few other things that you feel you can improve. Anyone else who has a supportive comment, please put it in, because we all deserve it at this point" ... After a few weeks, they realized what balance was. Then I could see the activities. They started going back in and start tweaking. I said, "So next week's thing is you're going to go back in and tweak the balance of your own recording and clean it up that way but use the same recording tracks that you have. If you feel you could do a better take over the last four bars throw that in" ... They understood perception of sound, what does sound sit in the whole scheme of things. Soundtrap was a big learning curve. We had lots of resistance, but I recorded myself singing every single line and it was not the best take. I used that to edit because I was thought if I'm hearing all their voices, they should hear me in my pandemic voice ...

One thing that was really interesting that I co-opted from my friend Elaine was the idea of this colored armband or wristbands. We gave them little welcome packs with hand sanitizer, masks (extra one), and three different colored bands: One green, one yellow, and one red. We put a little cue card in there that you [should] wear a different one or your preferred one every week. Green meant "I'm comfortable giving you hugs and high fives" and yellow was "Elbow bumps are great." And then red was "I'm happy to greet you from six feet away." So, everyone wore their own. No questions and no judgment because it was so hard when we couldn't see people's faces. We didn't know whether we should high five. "No? Yes?" Personal rejection—we didn't want to waste time with our brain power. [We] just wanted to go in and sing, so we took those guestimations out and it just ended up being so helpful.

Ferdinand: When I was at Oakwood [University] with the Aeolians, the Voces8 series would reach out to groups all over the world. They asked the Aeolians to do that Christmas Festival[8] and we did. Honestly, that Christmas special during COVID-19 kept the Aeolians going for that semester because that's all we did, the six or seven Christmas songs. All the groups throughout the world were taped wherever they were. Then you sent it off to Voces8, and they would involve ticket processing to your fan base and make this big project. Then people could buy the season pass where you could buy one of the videos. It was really well structured the way they had it. So, that kept the Aeolians going because as you remember, it was just so crazy. Some weeks, we just canceled rehearsal, depending on what was happening on campus. From August to the end of November, all we did were those six or seven Christmas songs, which seemed like it took an eternity to learn because of the pandemic and all the interruptions. But that festival really was ... the season for the Aeolians ... We did *We Shall Overcome*, the audio of which came from that recording that we did right before. We made *We Shall Overcome* part of the end-of-semester project, but everybody was already dispersed and home.

Collegiate Choirs—Reconceptualizing the Choral Rehearsal 67

How did you keep hope alive in your choir? What did you do to help your singers cope with not being able to sing?

Fox: It was the enrichment activities that we did that were really big and helped them stay connected. In March 2020, at the end of that year, the appreciation video projects happened. And then in the fall, we did the retirement home music video projects … Starting in the fall of 2020, we had to be separated with face shields and masks so they could see each other and hear each other. But I was able to help try to facilitate some community building experiences via Flipgrid. I made choir families. We would have rehearsals online, but they were not musicing during rehearsals. I created mad libs … so that they got to know a little bit more about people who they couldn't be next to in their own sections. They might not even know the names of people in their sections if we didn't use Flipgrid. What I saw happening among our choir folks on social [media] was rooted in grief, and rightfully so. A large part of our life was uprooted but things were seen from the standpoint of an administrator. I knew I, we, had to lead the way for keeping choral music alive.

Thomas: How did we stimulate interest during the rehearsals? We had a sectional time. I always had a speaker. I called on everybody to come in and speak to the choir. Among the guests were Anton Armstrong, Dale Warland, Lynne Gackle, Pearl Shangkuan, Eric Nelson, Mari Valverde, Rosephanye Powell, and Joel Thompson. At that time, I was doing a piece by Joel, a Yale student who spoke about his composition. Most guests either talked about their compositions, a composition we were performing, or other general topics. For example, Lynne Gackle discussed the aging singer. The choir was free to ask questions.

Harper: One thing that helped in fall 2020 and spring 2021, that entire year, we probably had about 15 guest speakers come in. So, there were days when they weren't singing or rehearsing. They were just sitting and listening to people talk. We had people from all over the world come in and that helped. In one of the virtual choir projects also in that fall semester, more people were struggling. We partnered with a choir from the National University of Costa Rica Choir, and so we had some Zoom social hours and that was nice. But at the end of the day, that fall semester particularly was really rough … Primarily, we had the two virtual choir concerts at the end of fall 2020[9] and at the end of spring 2021[10]. We tried to advertise them as much as possible. We made them events. I became an iMovie expert trying to put videos together and everything and make it look fancy. They really got on board.

Babb: I brought in the composer of *Arirang* [Sunkyong Lee] and let her tell her story, which was really touching and just amazing. It made them sing that piece entirely differently because *Arirang* was Korea's home song but then it got appropriated and then it got morphed and changed. Then it became something that was more militant and more showing pride in your country. She said, "*Arirang* is how we conquer the hardships in our life." She just was so, so sweet and special talking to the kids that they just fell in love with her, and they fell in love with the music. And finding those kinds of moments where they can really connect to the text and to each other, where they get to talk. So, I'm really into "Let's really dig into this text and talk about what it means, what it means to us individually, and what it means to us as a group. What do we want our story to be?"

How did the COVID-19 pandemic affect your programming?

Wong: Yes, partly for physical stamina and partly for mental well-being, and also for time, either rehearsal time or space, and when the concepts are going to be. It's just managing all the variables, and not really what I feel about the pandemic and that's how it's not a "me" program. Basically, it's how I can best manage everyone and people in a room. An SATB choir can sing in unison, and that is okay and there's nothing bad about it. We're building tone. If we start a rehearsal with that and we do it beautifully, I think that's a big win to build voices back, especially when we come back after a summer. I usually think, "Okay, let's sing in parts coming out of Summer," but now I know, "Okay, we just want to sing to be happy" …

Music that considers various talking points as well because not only has the pandemic been all about the health situation. But we have so much social commentary that's been going around that people are also thinking seriously about (and sometimes overthinking) because we had the time to do it. So, using time, not just for pure singing purposes, but also for discussions like what we would have online or choir and how important it is to have people chat with each other … I just realized that was so important to do … The word "diverse" is so overused now it's a buzzword, but it's also important to understand what diversity means in terms of programming for singers. I think because in the forefront, it would be all mostly from a cultural perspective but diverse opinions, text resources, composers, and lived experiences are totally different things. So, trying to expand what diversity looks at would be good, too ... I think we're done with too many pieces that are melancholic and lamenting. We have lots of new music coming out from the pandemic that is lamenting and very melancholic. It'll be nice to have a balance ...

Fox: It affirmed that what I was doing [pre-COVID-19] as a collegiate conductor-teacher was good enough, valid, and needed. I looked out and saw lots of people programming "difficult" and "highbrow" music that is often used to build a hierarchy among collegiate programs. I'd say to myself, "You know, why haven't I done a Bach motet? Why I haven't done this piece? I haven't done that piece." But it's okay that I am being who I am and who I need to be for the students in front of me right now. That's all that matters. I don't need to do certain repertoire to be able to say that our program is thriving and that we have wonderful musicians. I'm not only interested in helping support and sustain the great musicianship but more importantly, I want to help people be good to each other. I want to help them develop empathy because it is going to be an integral part of how we learn to be a better community to and for each other.

What new skills did you have to learn during the pandemic?

Fryling: I had some facility with GarageBand for sure, a little bit. I knew the concept of it, and I'd done a little bit of live stuff. I had used iMovie. I was an early adopter of iMovie when iMac came out. When my wife and I had children, I would make videos for them. It's pretty ... just drag and drop but then I moved to Logic and Final Cut Pro, which are based on iMovie and GarageBand, but they're just a different world ... I spent a lot of time on YouTube. There's a bunch of resources. At this point, I don't even remember. There was somebody who posted some stuff, and it was usually really basic, but then they would do a nice bibliography of, "If you really want to dig in, follow these links." There are a number of tutorials on YouTube that you could spend hours on, which I did. This piano behind me ... I bought that when I was a grad student because I needed a piano in Ann Arbor. It's not great, but it is weighted and makes a lot of noise when you play it, but it's also MIDI-capable. I'd never actually used the MIDI-capable part of it, so I learned how to do that. I had to get the special adapter because it's not a USB.

Wong: I learned how to use Zoom and all this extra stuff and acquired software and programs that I never needed before. Acquiring

	digital versions of music was the other thing that I had to do. It was a steep learning curve for me, even as a composer-arranger. Now digital copies, doing recordings, sync rights, "What does that mean?" Then, "What does that mean as a composer?"

Fox: My creativity turned up big time. I started the Professional Choral Collective (PCC)[11] during the summer of 2020. I wanted to bring music educators from around the world together to collaboratively chart a path forward in the pandemic when it looked like there was no way. These resources would be available to guide our colleagues who were grieving during the pandemic and also help our administrators learn how to best support us through this challenging time. Through the PCC, we were able to create a little over 100 different free learning activities for people to use. I reached out to six people with whom I am friends and I said, "Hey, I have this idea. I need you to be a facilitator. Here's how you facilitate. I'm getting people together to figure out how to do choir in a pandemic." They all agreed and off we went into uncharted territory. I was surprised to know the Country Music Association Foundation heard of my work and I was even more shocked when they invited me to help them create their *Unified Voices for Music Education*[12] project, which was based on my model for the PCC.

Is there anything you did or learned during the pandemic that you would keep post-pandemic?

Ferdinand: I learned a lot. I thought I rehearsed fast before the pandemic and people told me I typically do, but the pandemic taught me how to be way more efficient. Before I left Oakwood, the Aeolians for that last full year 2020–2021, I remember when we couldn't rehearse more than 30 minutes or whatever it was. Oh, man. It was lickety-split. So, even beyond the middle of the pandemic, even now I finish rehearsal long before the time—not long before every time, but you learn how to move things along. I'm going to keep that for the rest of my life. Efficiency was the name of the game, and rehearsing in 30 minutes, and just trying to get everything done. So, I'll definitely be keeping that.

Something I really didn't like before the pandemic, and I still kind of squirm a little bit about it—this whole notion of making part tracks. I'm not a part track guy. I want to do it the old-school way, but that was a lifesaver during the pandemic. For my pro group now, we don't do it for every song all the time, but it does help to give them a sense of reference. So, when we come together, they're like, "Okay, I kind of know how this is supposed to go." So, that's going to remain on some level, I think as long as you know how to go beyond these metronomic trappings.

I think the pandemic taught us ... well, for me, it taught me how to listen a different way. All the people who had to rehearse in a park, and decks, and outside. We got to rehearse in a basketball gymnasium. For the first two months, I had no idea what was going on. We couldn't hear anything—forget being on tempo and being on time. There was no such thing but then after a month or so you realize, "Wait, I'm not fussing with tempos anyways." You kind of get used to the space ... So, the pandemic taught us to listen a whole different type of way because we are creatures of our environment, right? We have to kind of be malleable. So, that taught us how to kind of suck it up when you get a bad room or try to figure out a room and all that.... And we were constantly changing. I remember some days I would be outside. Some days I was in the gym. It was just crazy.

Fox: In that time when we were in masks and face shields, students couldn't hear each other and what they've told me is that they actually had to listen to themselves more. So, when we took the face shields and masks away, my choir was better because they were better independent musicians. They were talking about their personal musicianship growth. Many of them said to me that because they couldn't hear anybody else, they were so focused on their own personal musicianship that they became stronger singers. I've had the best choirs since we've been through this pandemic. They just are singing better. We're learning music faster. They're more independent rhythmically, tonally, and responsible in terms of learning music on their own. It's just been fascinating. What I learned from the pandemic is rooted in the importance of challenging students to achieve beyond what they can envision and actively teaching the skill of perseverance. These things can empower students not only in our music learning spaces but also in life.

Babb: Having Zoom sectionals is a good thing to make my section leaders have to do some of that. It totally helps the ones who had to do that, and then they had to go student-teach in it ... The pandemic really forced me to step back away from the demands of a concert and to think about, "What do I really want to do with all of this time and all this rep?" I don't know if I really want to cram all this rep in just to say, "Ooh look when we did this new big shiny new thing!" Let's spend some time digging into the rep. And even though we have a concert every three or four weeks, let's do less but spend more time with it. I think that has been a big takeaway for me.

Harper: I don't know if it's so much patience because I think, as conductors, we all have a certain line we have to draw with expectations, attendance policies, and these kinds of things. But I certainly am more aware and sensitive to the fact that when students choose to share that maybe they're struggling or dealing with something, it's not just real but maybe a cry for help. I'm much more proactive now than I ever was about setting aside a lot of time contacting everybody making sure the student is aware of their options. One thing a student at LMU sometimes is not aware of is when they make a request for professional help or even to see somebody, that actually is something that can help safeguard them academically because now there's an official record that they have actually sought help, not just in an informal way.

Fryling: I think it was just generally that the important thing is to maintain a sense of hope and community. When we're together and able to sing, we do that by creating music with the idea of singing in a concert. When we were unable to do that, that was not motivating for anyone. I think that, for us, the healthiest thing was to let it go. We held on to it for a long time. In spring 2020, we were like, oh, full in the virtual stuff. Fall of 2020 as we started, we were like, "We're going to rock this virtual stuff!"[13-15] And we just very clearly fell apart by just listening to our recordings. The students weren't whining about the work ... I had a conversation over Zoom, one-on-ones, where the students were crying. Students were just really traumatized, and the last thing they needed was something else to learn, which they then had to sing while their roommate was in the room. It was kind of tough. So, I think that what I learned was (or reinforced—I think I've always known this) that we needed to aim for maintaining a goal of a hopeful learning community—that it's not always about "we have to achieve X because X is important." It's because it's a hopeful goal. It's something you want to do, and we do it together. Those three words: "Hopeful learning community," did not jibe with producing whatever we wanted to

	call it, virtual or nonvirtual singing into an empty hall. That was the students very much leading that direction.
Wong:	Zoom is a good backup if, say, suddenly, we cannot be in person. I can do something else, and we have Zoom ready to go … Something that I'll keep definitely is Zoom and the understanding of flexibility … We have always been practicing the choral art in person with pieces of paper that I feel I may have shut out so many other possibilities of connecting with people. But, of course, recognizing certain things cannot be replaced.
Robertson:	I'm much more apt to use some of the tech stuff I learned, but it's not the audio and video side. I use Google Forms, Google Slides, and Canva a lot more because it was what I communicated with…. Also, I talked to many choral directors who thought, "Oh, it's about the music." I don't think it is … It's about the people working together, making a community, building friendships. That's what makes the music beautiful and enjoyable for our audiences and our choir membership … I felt like being together singing was the "it," and virtual choir was just a stopgap. This was confirmed for me more than any other control experiment: What matters is being in the room, together and making music together. That's what matters.
Willer:	The other thing I am going to do every year—I'm doing all my fall auditions virtually because I can have them all in by the first of August and get all my listening done so they have their music by mid-August, and they can prepare for their first rehearsals. We're only doing in-person auditions at semester break, so all new students will do virtual auditions going forward. It's time saving but I also think it's a good experience for students to put together recordings. My auditions have two phases. First, they submit recordings of solo rep and then I ask for two vocalises so I can hear their range and also their flexibility of both long tones and agility. And then they have a synchronous audition online, where they have a prepared excerpt that they sing polyphony with a track of all the other parts. Then they do a bit of sight reading and tonal memory. And so, I have an eight-minute video of them doing their synchronous audition, which I watch along with their pre-recorded materials. And so, I can go back and re-reference it. In fact, it's really great for that first year and after that I see them in person at the end of the semester, and again at the end of the year. It's just those first-year students. I get a bigger picture of what they can do than I could get in a 10-minute audition …

It really made me appreciate what we do. I don't think choral music is going away any time soon. I just feel like we just got a really strong reminder of why it's important to make music with other people in person. [Laughs] And I think the kids got that too, not just the pros. They value it on a different level, at least my music majors do, than they did before ... We won't have that again hopefully, but I do think those are special kids. I think the ones who toughed it out are going to be different kinds of musicians down the road, which if there had to be a silver lining, I think that's probably what it is.

Is there anything else you want to say about how the pandemic has affected choral singing?

Eugene Rogers: COVID-19 has affected the academy's numbers. At the Univeristy of Michigan, we've got good people, but we don't have as many as we used to have singing in the choirs and majoring in voice. A lot of people were afraid to take that plunge because they saw how instantly professional singing work dried up.... I talked to a professional freelance artist who said they started a nursing degree during COVID-19 because all of their work dried up. We're going to feel a dearth in 5–10 years of professional singers. That's the side effect of COVID-19, the reality that the arts are very fragile if we have a major crisis. Sadly, as much as we know people need it, the world doesn't know how much they need it.

Without prompting, some conductors reflected on positive moments from the pandemic:

Dower: We do have classes on campus now, but our schedule is still probably about 50% remote. Students, we've found, have a preference, at least right now, even in the division of Visual and Performing Arts for some of their survey kind of history of classes. They have a preference for having those online so they can take them and still have a job. We are starting to recognize that trend and maybe we pivot those things. What I've also found, which is so interesting, is that we don't have the room space problem that we had prior to the pandemic. Now that 50% of those survey courses are fully online, I now have rooms available, large ones.

Willer: I'll never have this again. As a new professor at a new institution, I knew the individual voices of my students so well after that year. Going into my first year in person, I was like, "Wow, I know every kid and where their passaggio is, what kind of rhythms they're bad at." And it was such a great way to enter a job because that's the hardest year when you have to learn everybody's voice, and every year after that it's just the first-year class.

Wong: All of them were just so earnest. I always thought that the choral singers who have to do these sorts of ensembles [virtual] would do it pretty half-hearted. I was so wrong and throughout the whole pandemic even when we were in the throes of it, I've never not heard anything that was not done in earnest, so that is my bad for not thinking so highly. They knew that they had to do it and they begrudgingly did it, but the moment they did, it was the best singing. Or they just wanted to put the best version of themselves out there. No one's doing it half-assed basically, so I'm just really thankful for the singers. They just want to do well, and they'll figure it out.

Harper: One thing I will say is that we were fortunate…. Even in the fall of 2020 and spring of 2021, when we presented the virtual concerts and then also when we came back in person, the families and the university community were crazy supportive. I think that helped to legitimize or to help just the students feel like, "Okay, it wasn't all a waste of time. It was worth it." And so, that really helped us … I'm very proud of our profession, any one of the performative arts. We have colleagues in dance and theater, and the fact that we didn't totally lose our programs and that there wasn't a complete collapse speaks volumes to how hard we all worked and how much we truly are trying to be there for our students.

Notes

1 Oregon State University Bella Voce Treble Choir directed by Sandra Babb, *2021 ACDA National Conference Performance*, https://youtu.be/Ja71lbbDq3I
2 University of Nebraska at Omaha, *One Voice*, https://youtu.be/dJwEZiJeBQU?si=muNNkuRxk3Azt4SD
3 Loyola Marymount University, Los Angeles and Universidad Nacional, Costa Rica combined choirs, *You Do Not Walk Alone*, https://youtu.be/xyWfHgMtQuA?si=5g5cr9TuDL24oy7-
4 Tarleton University Choral Program, *Virtual Choir Performances*, https://youtube.com/playlist?list=PLLWh7wLsQ3c6elH517lwGXZ3Na-W-1byK&si=sO-fwBwOp8UCuzi0

5 Chor Amor, https://www.choramor.com
6 McMaster University Choirs, *World on Our Shoulders*, https://youtu.be/Ju9X2obeTjo?si=5xHQrSCidVGwBC0V
7 McMaster University Choirs, *Nyon Nyon*, https://youtu.be/6uA4Mxy5zlE?si=8pXiV_rMrewvZwCR
8 Live From London Christmas Highlights, *VOCES8 & Roderick Williams and The Aeolians*, https://youtu.be/xD7QZgWlO9M
9 Loyola Marymount University, *Winter Choral Concert 2020*, https://youtu.be/mM6-mddL_l4?si=NHAiyhv7xRK9cj0s
10 Loyola Marymount University Choirs, *Spring Cabaret 2021*, https://youtu.be/Begre_JKWrQ?si=BaJwZqWtLms18vW6
11 The Professional Choral Collective, https://www.drderrickfox.com/the-professional-choral-collective
12 Country Music Association Foundation, *United Voices for Music Education*, https://cmafoundation.org/resources/learn/
13 The Hofstra University Chorale Singers, *Pure Imagination*, https://youtu.be/Sp3tYHX_UlU?si=IBL69ojwmp9lVBJZ
14 The Hofstra University Chorale Singers, *Barber of Seville*, https://youtu.be/YjqEkYopiIo?si=_QzIWforRQEUMVPW
15 The Hofstra University Virtual Chorale, *Immortal Bach*, https://youtu.be/F9Noo80oPng?si=XTQXPCo_e11-5vt5

4 Professional Singers
Grief and Innovation

Interviewees

Sarah Brailey, Soprano; Director of Vocal Studies, The University of Chicago
Adam Faruqi, Tenor
Crossley Hawn, Soprano
Stephen Lancaster, Baritone; Associate Professor of the Practice and Head of the Graduate Voice Studio, University of Notre Dame
Kate Maroney, Mezzo-soprano; Voice Faculty, Mannes School of Music; Voice Instructor, Yale University

Introduction

Professional singers are masters of their art and craft their careers according to their strengths. They may give intimate solo recitals, collaborate in a chamber ensemble, and headline choral-orchestral concerts as featured soloists. They may serve as section leaders within an amateur chorus or sing in an entirely professional ensemble. Their commute may involve driving across town for weekly rehearsals or flying across the country for a two-week project with various choirs. With the advent of COVID-19, concerts were delayed and then canceled, necessitating the canceling or modifying of singers' contracts. Singing artists were left in a precarious position as freelancers and faced the possible end of their careers. This chapter focuses on five professional singers who responded to their loss of income with innovation and new ways of music-making. Their new pathways forged during the pandemic resulted in fulfilling new artistic ventures.

What were your musical plans when the COVID-19 pandemic emerged in March 2020?

Crossley Hawn: My spring of 2020 was going to be pretty busy with choral stuff. I had stuff with Cathedra, the Washington National Cathedral's chamber ensemble. I had

DOI: 10.4324/9781003330486-5

stuff with Bach Consort lined up, lots of choral gigs, and then I had three or four kinds of bigger solo things, too. I remember the day. There was one day when everybody canceled. I think they all heard that each other was [canceling] ... It was like, "They're canceling. We should probably cancel." Okay, so from the morning that day to the evening, I had lost thousands and thousands of dollars [Laughs] of work. I will say that many of the ensembles either that day or the next day said, "We will pay either your full fee or half of your fee, or you can elect to take your fee," so I was really fortunate that only a few things were really fully lost. It was just like, "Oh, God. Yeah, that was a stressful day [Laughs]." ... There was a lot of rescheduling or, like, "We'll pay you for the gig that was in April, but we can't pay you for the gig that's in May if things continue to get [worse] ..." because there was the two-week [Laughs] flattening of the curve that we were going to do.

Adam Faruqi: Well, everything dried up pretty much instantly. [Los Angeles] Master Chorale's whole season was canceled, as was LA Opera's, as was the Industry's. PRISM was put on hold. Tonality was put on hold. So right away in March, there was nothing and it looked like that would be the foreseeable future. There was a little bit of relief. The Master Chorale, for example, paid us COVID-19 Relief payments, which was very nice of them, facilitated through donations from their large donor base, which was a little bit of help.

Stephen Lancaster: What I went through, all professional singers went through; everything was canceled. There was definitely a feeling of really losing not only planned gigs; there were no gigs in sight. Some gigs were tentatively rescheduled for the following year, like AMF [Atlantic Music Festival]. My recitals in France were tentatively rescheduled, but my pianist and I [Laure Colladant] lost our American Church in Paris recital because that was planned five years out. With Conspirare, everything was supposed to be rescheduled to the following year. So, you were facing a whole year of nothing.

Kate Maroney: I remember, it was March, and everything through ... at first, it was through May, and then through June

	[got canceled]. But Santa Fe [Desert Chorale], we didn't know about their July [performances] for a little while. Within a matter of 48 hours in that week in March, basically, the next four months were canceled. [My husband] Red and I went up to Rochester and stayed with my in-laws for a few months. But then, of course, probably by April and May, the Desert Chorale knew that we weren't going to be able to do that. And then, I had things through the fall, and I had Messiahs and all. Then, as things kept rolling along, everything really started getting canceled through all of 2020.
Sarah Brailey:	I was supposed to do *Ich Habe Genug* and some arias from a Handel oratorio with the Minnesota Bach Ensemble. They canceled two hours before the concert. I think it was the 13th of March. I was in the Twin Cities and got the email. I drove home and entered quarantine because the governor of Minnesota had just declared a limit on in-person events.

What challenges did you have to overcome? How did your focus and plans change to meet those challenges?

Hawn:	There were a couple of days of spiraling. After that, I was in a very fortunate position, actually. At the National Shrine, my boss's executive assistant needed to move to part-time because she had young children who were home from school now, so she needed help. I got an email from the rector of the Shrine. It was just like, "Hey, I've heard from the music director that singers are not doing so hot right now. Would you be interested in some part-time office work?" I was like, "Yes! Anything! Please give me a job." I took over there and worked some hours at the Shrine, which really helped. The Shrine Choir was reduced from 25 people down to five, and we were 10 or 12 feet apart in the chancel. We're really lucky because that space is ginormous. Even when there was nobody in the congregation, we were able to spread out for tapings of masses.[1] I actually never stopped working in the church. It was reduced, what we were doing, for sure, but there was sort of that constant stream of money for me, which I was very fortunate to have.... We did tapings of services. Then they were letting 100 people for a little while, and then 250 people for a little while, but it was definitely very strange to be

doing. We did Holy Week in 2020 with nobody in the Shrine. It's usually 5,000 people in there, and it's just like empty, with five of us singing. I gotta tell you, it was actually the most special Holy Week [Laughs] ever....

I also applied to some of the artist grants ... You basically just put in how much work and how much money you had lost in the spring season, and then they gave you grants based on that. That was also incredibly helpful, too.

I guess I'm kind of incapable of just chilling out. I'm incredibly Type A [Laughs], so when all of my projects got canceled, I was like, "Ah, need creative outlet. Must do something." I thought, "Okay, well, I've heard of Patreon. I've heard of people taking song requests, which might be really kind of fun, actually." I did some research on the platform and decided to launch a page. Allan [husband] kind of really encouraged me to do that, too. I was like, "Are people going to want to be hearing songs right now, or is everyone going to be like, 'Please shut up'?" [Laughs] I don't know, but he kind of convinced me. He was like, "No, I think people need art right now," and I was like, "Okay." I started a Patreon page,[2] which was kind of a hodgepodge of all different styles of music because I was basically just taking any kinds of song requests. I did everything from folk and pop music to country and then, of course, classical. It was just actually great because I come from a pop-rock background....

He [Allan] helped me a lot on these creative projects that I was doing for Patreon. I'm useless on the computer. I don't know anything about sound editing or video editing. He was like my knight in shining armor for technology. [Laughs] ... We turned our office into a recording studio. Allan built a really nice mic, and we got good speakers. This wooden thing behind us, we surround [ourselves with it] and then drop towels and blankets. Then I have a stand with towels and blankets, so it's creating a little box....

It was really fun for me to just be at home learning my ukulele and playing piano again and recording pop songs and lots of folk stuff. It was definitely kind of my emotional saving grace through the whole thing because I got to keep working, essentially. It looked very different, but I had something that was giving me some artistic purpose through the whole thing.... I was overwhelmed by the support I received. I think a lot of folks in the corporate world, or in worlds where their job was safe and they just worked from home, they really stepped up and supported the arts in that time, at least in my sort of little community. It was overwhelming, especially in the beginning. It's like, "Thanks, guys." [Laughs] ...

Thinking about singing during the pandemic versus sort of the live singing that we're starting to do again, was just how different the singing felt. When you had a microphone right here in your face, it was difficult to sing in the same way that you would've sung. There was a lot of trust that went into your sound editor. Like, "Please, please add reverb to this. Please take out my disgusting mouth noises that, somehow, I just make three times as many as every other person on the planet." [Laughs] There was that element of it feeling incredibly intimate, especially for the virtual recordings where you're sending in your stuff and they're layering a thousand things. The hardest part of that part of the pandemic for me was just feeling like this and really needing to get over the mental hurdle of, "No, just sing, Crossley. Just sing" [Laughs].

Faruqi: Primarily what kept me alive was my church gig, surprisingly. They doubled my pay during the pandemic and demanded more than double the work. Prior to the pandemic, we were going in twice a week, Thursday night rehearsals and Sunday morning services, and singing, and that's it. But during the pandemic, they assembled a production team among whom I was a member and we produced two music videos a week for them. It was a lot of work—some were more work than others. Some of them were just taking four-part hymns from the hymnal and recording multi-tracks and then stringing them together. Some of them were custom arrangements with a lot of different moving parts, but that really kept me alive. That mixed with unemployment was the only reason I was able to stay in my apartment and didn't become homeless and was able to buy food....

[We were] completely virtual for many, many months. Eventually, after maybe five or six months, we did go into the church and around the church as well. This was part of my duties. What you're looking at me on right now is my DSLR. I would go to the church and take pictures and film time-lapse footage and all kinds of stuff to incorporate into these music videos. I had the time to do it, you know, I wasn't [Laugh] doing anything else, but it was nice. Not only did it pay me, but it kept me busy. It gave me something to do to keep me sane....

I really had to diversify and expand what I do... As a kid, I noodled around and made funny little videos and put them on YouTube and that sort of thing, just as a hobby. I guess the pandemic forced me to monetize it.... There were a few film and video game soundtracks that wrapped up their production at the beginning of the pandemic. It was really interesting how that sort of adapted to singing at home because some of these projects were done right here, like in my bed. I was singing Wow! [Laugh] and coordinating with 40 people via emails and click tracks and everything. It was very challenging and fascinating.... And also, the way that opened up has changed. At first, everyone was singing in the studios in plexiglass booths with their own individual microphones. It was limited to 8, 10, 16 people and then gradually the numbers increased. Gradually, the booths went away and now it's almost pretty much back to full capacity with PCR (Polymerase Chain Reaction) testing the day before and rapid testing the day of. The film studios have the most rigorous testing mandates out of every institution I sing for.

Maroney: I think by the fall [of 2020], we were doing a lot of Zoom church services. At St. Ignatius Loyola,[3] which is my Sunday morning gig, we did weekly Zoom recordings and I continued to be paid. Then I also did work for Holy Trinity Bach Vespers[4] where I've sung also. I've worked with them for about a decade. We were doing a lot of virtual stuff. It seemed, by the fall of 2020, that I was still having income from these things. I think I was sort of in a rarefied group of the New York City people who were working in places that had the institutional support to keep their 12 singers paid weekly for doing Zoom anthems and motets, which is less than ideal, but I really did that all of fall 2020 into 2021. We were all recording individually at home using iPhones. At St. Ignatius, it would be like a hymn or two every week. We got into a routine of doing it, but it was every week. Everyone could record at any time and there was always a due date. So, it would be due like on Wednesday morning before the weekend. And then the music staff, at St. Ignatius, it was Bobby Reuter (Trinity was doing similar things), people would put together those virtual choir videos every week. There's a whole archive. I mean, Scott Warren at St. Ignatius had said, "If we have to go back to doing that, I'm not going to make people record because we're just going to draw from what we already recorded." There are all these videos of every different motet you think of, Renaissance polyphony, hymns, and it's just 16 heads ... We did so many of them.

I think it was probably so tedious for the people who were doing it.... There was so much trial and error at the beginning, too, and different people would be recording it in different ways. I remember distinctly that people were like, "Use your iPhone. That's actually the best quality mic. Position it this way" ... in order for them to kind of mix the voices. A few people got some very rarefied skill sets during that time because I'm sure they got better at the process. But it was incredibly time-consuming, and everyone seemed so burned out on it. I felt burnt out on having to sit and just sing the alto part ... At first, I was like, "Oh, this is so great! We have the solution, and it's still providing music." And then I came around to like, "This is not really making music. We're not singing in a room with other parts." You're trying to be very technically perfect and keep it in tune, and cutoffs and everything but it's not making music. I think that's generally the sentiment, although I'm grateful that I did that....

We were in my mom's house in New Jersey in the fall of 2020. We had some good microphones because my husband, Red, is a computer music guru. [He] really has all the good recording equipment and everything. I learned a little bit more about mics. It's not information I've retained but I guess I have learned about the optimal setup and the mic placement. For Seraphic Fire, I had to record the Brahms [piece] for three-part women's choir ... we had to do an audio recording separately and then lip-sync to the audio recording for the video, but it was just so complicated. Seraphic sent out this guide, and literally, it was like, "The best place may be going into a closet and recording, just because that gives us the most ability to blend the sound. You don't want to be in a reverberant space." We were in my childhood basement, where there was this big rug and a low ceiling, and that's where I recorded those Brahms songs. It was so bizarre and felt terrible—every little vocal flaw and everything. They're like, "Oh, you have to listen to it and then send it in," and you're like, "They're probably never going to hire me because these recordings are so raw." It was crazy, and in my apartment in New York, I mean, that's why the process became frustrating. I remember posting one thing because I got a perfect take of something, and then our cat meowed a split second after the end of it. All this funny stuff....

I had the help of a sound engineer background kind of husband. Other singers may have had to do more of it on their own with figuring out. I had my own system and process and now I feel comfortable doing it. But I never got the ring light or certain things that I know people really invested in for their home studios, and I probably should, honestly, because we may return ... And there was the argument that now we know we can do things on Zoom, which is actually kind of cool, even for this kind of meeting or for the future. If you're rehearsing with people and you have a schedule, maybe that very first rehearsal where you just talk about the music—maybe some of that can be done over Zoom. That's cool, but yeah, the learning curve was so steep for all of us, so we incorporated a lot of new things.

I sang some Schubert songs for the Brooklyn Art Song Society, and that was with the pianist. We went to his space, and we recorded it. But I've talked to other performers. I was performance-ready with the songs. They're memorized. You go out, but without that energy from an audience, it's so weird.... When something is being recorded, you know it's going to be around forever, so that's also a different kind of pressure that you feel when you're doing it. I hope we're past that, even if we now have another variant wave because that was definitely a good solid year of doing a lot of that kind of stuff....

I'll absolutely keep a KN95 [mask] on this weekend at St. Ignatius for all of Thursday, Friday, Saturday, and Sunday. I'm singing *Easter Oratorio* on Sunday at Holy Trinity. I'm singing the aria and everything. I don't think I'm going to take my mask off. I'm resolved to it being really difficult, and probably people not even hearing it that well, but I really don't want to get COVID-19 in the next couple of weeks. And singing with these masks, I have noticed, more so just recently, that I have some jaw tension. I feel like I need to go work with an Alexander Technique specialist or something, because ... it's terrible, and the pressure it puts on my nose ... I think when I'm wearing it, I'm always kind of popping my jaw ... and that seems like a universal thing.

Lancaster: I just lost the desire to learn any of that music or work on it. So, I had to ask myself, "What am I going to do?" There was nothing to perform, so I ended up filling the time with other things. I filled some time with things that I had never gotten around to, just regular life stuff. I spent some time trying to come up with new ideas, rethinking: "What's important to me as an artist? What projects do I want to do? What do I not want to do in the future? Who do I want to be?" Then the big thing that filled my time of course, as you know, was being an "academic." We gave so much more time to service, replanning, teaching online, and all of that. You knew you had the time, the university needed you, and the students needed you, so you just did it. We didn't get a summer off; we worked all through the summer on school stuff. Kiera [Duffy, University of Notre Dame colleague] was on maternity leave from March 2020 until mid-fall 2020, exactly when COVID-19 hit. She told me, "I'm so sorry!" She still helped me with all these things that summer, which she shouldn't have had to do....

Fall 2020 to spring 2021, that was all [teaching on] Zoom. The students were on campus. We had it a little bit better than most: They were able to give recitals in the spring of 2021 at long distances in person. The lessons were online. This year [2022], all the lessons have been in person with masks. Then in Spring 2021, that's when nothing was getting rescheduled for me. France got postponed again. That's the year I spent a lot of extra time coordinating AMF. They needed an online program, and they didn't know what to do. We did a hybrid program, which I had to create from scratch. [Still] no gigs in sight. I just ended up doing more things that I wouldn't normally have done....

Then [in] 2021, still, all solo gigs were canceled. My Conspirare gigs had been rescheduled again to 2022. At that point, I thought, "I really need to rethink what my professional career is supposed to be. I love Conspirare. I think I want to do more choral singing." Then I had a conversation with Eugene [Rogers], and I asked him, "Can I join EXIGENCE [Vocal Ensemble]? I'm a quarter Puerto Rican." He said, "Yes, technically you can. It depends on how you identify and what that means to you." I had to send in an audition video that included dancing, because some of the songs they sing are choreographed since they come from particular Black and Latinx music traditions. I auditioned for them in August of 2021. After that, he called me and said, "You're in. I've got a gig for you in January of 2022." He said, "We also just had people cancel for our October gig. Would you be willing to learn the whole program in two weeks?" I said, "Yes!" I had not performed since March 2020, so I thought, "I will take this gig and I will learn it in two weeks. I will do all of this." We performed in masks, of course, but that gig turned out to be life-changing. EXIGENCE is an amazing group; being part of it has helped me reconnect with my Latinx heritage.... Then it turned out the January gig had to be postponed to January 2023 because of Omicron. It's been fits and starts....

I mean, a similar thing happened with AMF. We were planning on an in-person program in the summer of 2021. Then there was that critical point where we had to decide, "Will we say 'yes' to in person? Or do we switch to online? Or do we try to do hybrid?" We decided to go hybrid, which meant that the opera production would be in-person, in a pod, and the institute would be online. Then I had to create a two-week online program out of thin air, which I had never done before. I spent hours on it; I'm very proud of what I did. At the time, I thought, "This is the future of education: Hybrid." So, I did all this work. It happened, and it was really good. Then when it was done, I thought, "I don't think we'll ever do this again."

Brailey: I was in the last year of my coursework for my doctorate, and I was a TA [teaching assistant]. We had to go online for all the voice lessons that I was teaching and figure out how to use Zoom. At that point, all my students had gone home because the University at first had just closed for two weeks and then obviously stayed closed. They were all at home and had iffy Wi-Fi. The lessons were very sporadic in quality or varied in quality because of the internet connection but at least I had that bit of income from my graduate stipend to rely on through June of 2020. That was the end of my TA position even though I had one more year to finish up my dissertation. In the beginning, several gigs paid most or all of my fees, which was amazing, so that helped tide me over for a while. Lorelei pretty quickly went into strategizing mode, "What can we do to support you guys?" So, [they] came up with a lot of different educational offerings. We did some masterclasses and teaching residencies with groups like the Pennsylvania Girl Choir. I spoke at Peabody [Institute] a few times. Lots of my friends and colleagues who have academic positions hired me for virtual masterclasses or career talks, which was really nice. That was very helpful. I didn't get unemployment from the State of Wisconsin because, of course, it's complicated as a freelancer and takes longer like six months. So, yeah, it was pretty stressful. Finally, the unemployment came through in the fall.

Around the same time, I was contacted by Matt Curtis. We grew up in the same town but never knew each other because he went to the Catholic High School. He's a couple of years younger than me, but I knew of him, and we were Facebook friends. I knew he had started this Choral Tracks company. He reached out and asked if I was available to do some recording and I said, "Yes, absolutely." So, at first, from

October to January, I was freelance and just as many hours as I wanted. And then January 2021, he hired me full-time. So, I had a salary job with vacation time. He really saved me, and I can do it all remotely from here. I'm still doing it part-time when I have free time.... I did take one day, and I went to Matt's. He gave me a mic, mic stand, external monitor, audio interface, and software and showed me how to do it. We share everything through Dropbox. I have like a to-do folder. I can just record at my leisure. I forget how many staff people he has now, but he has enough that whenever I have a question, somebody's always available. Before I started Choral Tracks, I also invested in a couple of microphones and an audio interface and tried to figure out how to do all that. So, yeah, new skills....

Then, in the spring, my teacher's wife saw this listing, I think, on the NATS [National Association of Teachers of Singing] website for the position at the University of Chicago. It's a slightly unusual position because it's in addition to being the Director of Vocal Studies and teaching private voice lessons, it also supports the choral program. The job description was kind of perfect for me. So, even though I had thought, "I don't know if I'm ready for an academic job, especially in the middle of COVID-19," I thought, "Well, this sounds so perfect, and it's part time, so I could still gig. So, I might as well apply." They hired me. I just finished my first academic year as the Director of Vocal Studies. It's two days a week. My sister lives in Chicago, so I drive down, teach, stay at my sister's, teach, and drive home. It's very flexible and my students, of course, are super smart. So, between those few bits of stable income, as gigs have started coming back, I felt a lot more secure than I did two years ago....

Handel and Haydn [Society] was really exceptional in trying to take care of its musicians financially. They did a one-time draw on their endowment to help pay out our contracts. I can't remember if they paid fully or a percentage, but they honored every contract to some extent. They also found lots of different ways to do virtual events, like Emily Marvosh started hosting concerts. She'd do like talkbacks and whatnot for the concert videos that they produce, which were high quality. They hired me to do some educational things. They have a high school scholarship, a couple of different scholarships, and so they asked me to adjudicate those and things like that. They really cared for us, which felt really nice.

What did you do to cope with not being able to sing? How did you keep hope alive?

Faruqi: I bought a bicycle. I went on daily rides around the Hollywood reservoir, which is maybe 10 minutes from here, some little lake. I went and took lots of photos of flowers and I connected with friends online. I played a lot of Animal Crossing. I more than tripled my plant collection.

Lancaster: I think [my husband] Kevin and I developed our own routine of happy hour each day. We would do our work, and then at a certain time every day, we would sit down, and we would have a drink together, and just chill. He would cook a wonderful dinner. In the summer, once the weather was warm enough, we were constantly on our friends' patios and sitting outside. We did as much socializing outside as we could possibly do. There were also a couple of my friends from my DMA [Doctor of Musical Arts] class at Michigan: Voice teachers. We began to Zoom every couple of months and just commiserate together about the pandemic protocols as teachers. Then Conspirare did something wonderful. They started having a Conspirare group Zoom once every three months or so. Those were wonderful. They were just big groups of people on Zoom. There would be an open time for sharing what people were going through. It was actually so comforting to hear how everyone was having a hard time. Some people were having really hard times. There was always someone on that Zoom who was having a worse time than you. It was an opportunity to really all "be together" and share in the misery. Then we would listen to some music. That was really nice. I reconnected with lots of people during that time, as we all did. That was good. I think that kept hope alive until maybe the winter of 2021. Then we got the vaccines. That seemed to make things better. I do remember feeling like most of 2020 was really tough. You had already exhausted all of the new "online" ideas and you were facing another year of not performing.

Brailey: Eventually I was okay. I finished teaching as a TA. Those next few months were rough. I also lost my dad in August of 2020. So that was really rough. There was a lot of grief. I became obsessed with plants [Laugh]. That was really honestly therapy. I'd never really had plants before because I travel so much, and I figured I couldn't keep them alive. I just got really upset and some people sent condolence plants when my dad passed. I have like hundreds of houseplants now. I also bought a house a year ago. I've been doing a lot of outdoor gardening now and yeah, that's been really therapeutic. In the beginning, of course, we did a lot of Zooms with friends. My best friend's mom lives in Madison, so we did a weekly outdoor dinner even through December in Wisconsin. We bundled up and she would make hot sandwiches wrapped in foil so we could eat them with our mittens on and some sort of hot spice wine or cider. I think we did that down to mid-20 degrees [Laughs].... And I sort of got used to the uncertainty of whether things were going to happen or not. But at first, it was really traumatic. I mean, I had some cancellations, like some of the best gigs in my life that I cried over because I was like, "Is my career over?"

Hawn: It was really interesting talking to some of my singer friends who just temporarily turned off that part of themselves. I totally get why they did that and why they needed to do that to sort of preserve emotionally. I had the opposite kind of thing. I needed to sing. Again, I was really, really lucky because I was singing almost every week at the Shrine, still, both sort of the canting of them, the TV masses, and also in these quintets. My job changed. We went from four or five people a section, kind of an easy, breezy church job, to, like, "Okay, you're alone on a part every day, so good luck [Laughs] and it's being broadcast to thousands and thousands of people." It got more stressful, which helped me not to be complacent. [Laughs] I had to stay on my toes through the pandemic, musically. I think, for me, I never really sort of lost that hope or that musical drive, because I just was in a position of continuing to do it in a different way.

Maroney: I always kind of had little things to work toward, but I do think, looking back, I'm probably in this rare group of people, just by virtue of being so diversified in kind of what I do, that I still had things. But that first spring, when everything really shut down, including Baldwin Wallace [University], I remember kind of feeling a freedom so I could practice whatever I wanted. We were at my in-laws and my son was 15 months at the time, but they were spending time with them. In a weird way, our day to day was so much easier than I think people whose children were a little bit older, or who didn't have that family support. So, I was practicing Bach. I was trying to practice piano skills. I was playing preludes and fugues, like one hand at a time, just sort of trying. I was singing a lot of rep and just sort of having fun that I could practice anything—our old Faure songs that I hadn't sung in forever. I was kind of just singing through stuff and in a weird way, it felt nice. I've talked to a few singers who feel this way but again, it's probably a privileged way to feel, but I almost feel like maybe I was doing too much before—too much that I was always kind of feeling like, "Okay, I have to be doing this this week, this this week, and preparing." Suddenly, when all of that went away, I still wanted to make music, but I could just kind of do whatever I wanted and that was really nice. I've talked to other singers who felt like, without having performance deadlines, they didn't feel the urge to practice. I totally get that, but I realized this about myself, I don't feel that way. In fact, I don't love performing as much as I love just exploring music and rehearsing, honestly. I get really nervous performing but going someplace in those first couple days of rehearsals, that's my favorite part of making music. So, in some sense, I didn't feel nervous or anxious about anything and I just kind of practiced whatever I wanted. But yeah, but it was scary because it was also kind of like, well, "Should we find other jobs? Or how long is this going to last?" So, I don't know. Those are my feelings about it and then we were taking walks. We were baking bread like Laura [Strickling, soprano]. There were other things that suddenly I had a little more space and time for and that was kind of nice.

Is there anything you did or learned during the pandemic that you would keep post-pandemic?

Faruqi: Well, a lot of that [virtual choir] work dried up after the lockdowns ended but I still use my audio engineering skills for my own projects. I learned so, so much and I hope to continue using them, if not in a professional capacity, then at least just for myself, to make my own music and to post it online and that sort of thing.

Brailey: Yeah, definitely in terms of practical things. I don't know if you have heard of this Julia Wolfe [piece, *Her Story*][5] that Lorelei is premiering. It's for ten voices. So, I just multitracked the soprano, the five soprano parts, and Eliza Bagg did the five alto parts. She [Wolfe] consented to the choreographer or the director to get a sense of the piece, the first two movements. She hasn't finished it all yet. That's super useful for her. It was very easy because I have a whole setup right here and

I was like, "Yeah, no problem. One afternoon, fine, done." [Laughter] So, yeah, knowing how to do that has been life changing, career changing, and just knowing that I have that as a fallback....

He [Matt] just bought a venue in Lacrosse. He's doing lots of amazing things. I'm really grateful to him and having that sense of cushion and stability is really nice, because who knows how long we're going to be with COVID-19, maybe forever. I sort of already started getting to this point in my career where ... I mean, it's part of why I left New York. I wanted more stability and I wanted to be able to really focus on what I wanted to do artistically and not just take gigs because I needed to pay my rent. I'd already started thinking about that and I think the pandemic intensified that because I really like my life in Madison, and I really like my students. I still love traveling and gigging, but I'm only going to do projects with people I really want to work with and music I really want to do. That lesson, I think, has just been solidified through the pandemic and I feel really lucky to be at a point in my career in life where I can make those decisions. I mean, I feel so intensely for students right now....

Hawn: I learned that I want to focus more on projects that I want to focus on. There was a lot of time management that went into the pandemic where it was like, "Okay, I am working on Patreon. I'm working on quintet singing, and then I'm doing a lot of virtual recordings for ensembles." It kind of taught me that, like, "Okay, I really care about these things. Maybe I don't need to be so involved in the grind when I get back." I've been trying, and sometimes failing, but trying to say "no" to a little bit more, just to preserve some creative juices. It was so nice to do some stuff that I wanted to do, especially on Patreon, and to have the space and the time to do those things which I never had before. I'm trying to keep a little bit of that moving forward, and things are really picking up again in [Washingon,] D.C. It's been, like, "Okay, Crossley, you told yourself that you were going to have [Laughs] some more time and some more headspace." Yeah, so time management for sure, sort of learning what things to make a priority.... "Oh, spending time at home with my husband is actually really great. This is lovely."

Lancaster: I think there's definitely now more of a positive sense of being back at it.... I'm excited and I'm finally motivated again now that I have gigs. I don't want to go back to normal in the sense of going back to just a busy life. I really, really want to try to make life more humane for myself. I'm not saying I'm succeeding.... I think it's letting go of guilt for purposefully doing less so that I can breathe and not be so stressed—refusing to feel guilty about doing less.... I will also say this. There are some things that I think have changed for the better. As a professional singer, I studied with David Jones in New York City. Pre-pandemic, I would go to take lessons from him once or twice a year. I would go for three or four days and take a lesson each day. Then with the pandemic, he had to move everything online and I've taken lessons with him once a month online. It's been great. I feel as a singer, that was my lifeline: My monthly voice lesson with him online. I kept feeling like I was progressing: Actually, a lot more than I did before when I would have to go in these spurts to New York City. That's been a good thing.

Maroney: Coming back out of it, you're thinking, "Well, I want to keep that kind of balance." I think a lot of singers I talked to, people were like, "Well, there are these other things that I value doing in life and I just hadn't prioritized [them] because I was so focused on trying to make a career" ... So, I think a lot of people have had to shift what's really important. It's different for everyone ... I think, ideally, that I'm not so crazy that I feel stressed where I'm like, "Oh, why did I say, 'yes' to all of these things?" because I think the pace of life I really enjoy. Again, my son, he'll be three-and-a-half pretty soon, and just wanting to make sure that I have time with him and time with our family. We were with our parents a lot, my mom, and my in-laws, and we've all, I think, wanted to really put a priority on making sure we block out these times where we can spend quality time and do other things. I started taking a French class this semester, which was so much fun, because I studied it for three or four years ago because I want to become better at it. I mean, that's not musical, it's related ... But I just think I just kind of want to do things that I can control my own intrinsic growth or something ... I mean, being a freelancer is great, but we all get used to this hustle mentality and "This is going on and how do I fit everything in?" I'm trying to let go of some of that. I don't want to return right back into that mentality because, well, I'm also going to be 40. I mean, maybe you feel that way more when you're in your 20's.... The pandemic slowed a lot of that down, and I want to keep that, if I can. Yeah, things don't have to be frenetic....

When all of this hit, I was thinking a lot about how maybe some major restructuring could happen in terms of (this has been a theme in many fields) freelancers and protection for artists. I wrote a piece that was just an op-ed in The Washington Post about the Federal Music Project after the Great Depression—how we really needed some sort of more safety for all of the people who just suddenly lost all income because of the way our contracts are structured, which sort of just put in no protections, and that was all at the beginning of the pandemic. Luckily, a lot of people do seem as though they were able to get some sort of pandemic relief, unemployment for a period of time. I know there are still Small Business Association loans that people are able to apply for and everything. But I think that a larger theme in our field is just the voice of freelance singers and freelance musicians not always being protected. Now what's emerged in this past year with every group having different protocols, different safety measures, different states having different regulations ... I feel like we're the ones who are left with fewer protections than any other part of putting music together. So, people get sick on gigs, and there's nothing kind of contractual often that indicates what will happen. Everyone's just been trying to figure it out as we go along. But I've been hoping that maybe there could be a guild established, maybe with ACDA. I've been in talks, because I am a member of AGMA (American Guild of Musical Artists), trying to kind of organize or unionize some professional choral organizations. Maybe that's a stretch, I don't know, but just something so that the workers have more collective bargaining power when it comes to contracts and things. For all of these groups, if the people in charge are wonderful, then you're treated really well and paid fairly. You know your accommodations are going to be okay. But then sometimes, we have these situations where those things aren't guaranteed. Now that I'm older, I'm really interested in helping to raise the bar for the whole industry so that people coming out of school who are always desperate to say "yes" to anything ... How do we put some protections in place? I don't have the solutions, but I have been in conversations with a lot of people about this kind of thing and I care about it....

The toxicity, that is something. I'm really committed personally to only working with people that I feel really comfortable with. There's been, I'm sure you've seen, especially in New York, just a shift recently, that I think maybe, hopefully, will help raise the culture and allow people to feel that they can speak up more freely without fear of retaliation if they feel like they've been harassed or abused in some way. Because there's just always been this fear, "Well, maybe I'm not going to get hired again if I say something," and it just can't happen.

Without prompting, some singers reflected on positive moments from the pandemic:

Lancaster: I had a CD that I had recorded in 2018, but it had not been sufficiently edited. When COVID-19 happened, I finally sat down and did all the edits. March 2020 to December 2020 was when all of that happened. I finished up a CD[6] because I finally had the time....

To me, teaching was the best part of COVID-19, not because it wasn't hard to deal with masks and teaching online—all of that was pretty difficult. Ultimately though, I didn't really feel that those changes were the most stressful thing for me. It was all the added admin and decision-making that was going on that was hard for me. Teaching fed back into me. It was the only thing that was feeding back. In other words, just being with students, seeing them all continue to improve, and feeling that I was helping someone: That was the most high-quality thing going on in my professional life and the most satisfying in an artistic way....

Faruqi: I got a lot better at audio engineering, video editing, and photography. In fact, because of the skills that I was able to gain as a part of this church production crew, I started getting other work doing audio engineering and video editing for other arts institutions in LA. For example, I did a virtual choir music video for Street Symphony.[7] I did one for the Master Chorale and smaller little clients like Pasadena Pro Musica.[8]

Is there anything else you want to say about singing through COVID-19?

Brailey: At the beginning of COVID-19, it was really traumatic for all performers who were just getting their work canceled outright and a lot of organizations didn't pay them. I can't say they didn't honor their contracts because the pandemic wasn't cited in force majeure. I get how, for organizations, force majeure also protects them from having to pay venue rental fees, etc. But I was hoping that there would be more changes across the board from hiring organizations in terms of "If something gets canceled, if it's X number, X amount of time before the concert, we'll pay you X percent of your contract," because, obviously, we've already started learning it. That has happened with some groups, but it's a little disheartening how a lot of groups have just gone back to business as usual …

What are you looking forward to as COVID-19 hopefully becomes endemic?

Brailey: I've done a lot of live concerts this season [2022]. I'd say starting in like November-ish things started to come back. For the most part, groups have been really good about having COVID-19 protocols and sharing those with the artists, so I felt pretty safe. I did get COVID-19 but not until like a month ago and it wasn't from a gig…. So, I'm leaving for a gig tomorrow. We have to test before we arrive, and we're masked everywhere except at rehearsals. There are different protocols for singers or wind players who will be unmasked on rehearsal. Places are being pretty conscientious, which makes me feel pretty safe. There's always some level of risk, but we want to make music [Laughter]….

In terms of what I'm looking forward to, my summer's a good mix of fun gigs and downtime. Lorelei's at Tanglewood a few times, which is always nice. I'm leaving tomorrow to go to The Bard Festival to do some David Lang chamber music. I feel like groups are still being a little bit more careful about future planning, so I don't have as much on my calendar as I normally would at this time for the next season, but that's okay because I know I'll be okay financially. There were a couple of times this season where I took everything because I was like, "Oh, my God, performing again!" And then when I was doing it, I was like, "Oh, this is exhausting. Maybe I shouldn't have agreed to travel for three weeks straight." But yeah, in general, it just feels really nice to return to some semblance of normalcy.

Notes

1 The National Shrine, *Sunday Mass*, https://www.youtube.com/@marysshrine
2 Crossley Hawn, *Patreon Page*, https://www.patreon.com/crossleyhawn
3 St. Ignatius Loyola, *Service Livestreams*, https://www.youtube.com/@StIgnatiusNYC/streams
4 Holy Trinity Lutheran Church, *Service Livestreams*, https://www.youtube.com/@holytrinitylutherannyc
5 Julia Wolfe, *Her Story*, https://www.loreleiensemble.com/wolfe
6 Stephen Lancaster, *Robert Schumann: Dichterliebe, Op. 48 and Liederkreis, Op. 39*, https://music.youtube.com/playlist?list=OLAK5uy_lglbJcrtUdBn9cFqon3vkWTq9ps5mdC0g
7 Street Symphony, *Cohen Hallelujah*, https://youtu.be/Z1qw7IFV8KE
8 Pasadena Pro Musica, *United We Sing*, https://youtu.be/QU8imUO6MoM

5 Professional Choirs
Reimagining the Art

Interviewees

Katherine FitzGibbon, Artistic Director, Resonance Ensemble
Joshua Habermann, Artistic Director, Santa Fe Desert Chorale
Craig Hella Johnson, Artistic Director, Conspirare
Donald Nally, Conductor, The Crossing
Eugene Rogers, Director, EXIGENCE
Beth Willer, Artistic Director, Lorelei Ensemble

Introduction

Professional choirs perform and commission works that propel the choral arts forward. They feature rosters of paid singers at the highest level of their craft. At the helm are conductors who push the boundaries of what is possible in the choral ensemble. When COVID-19 arrived on (and somewhat decimated) the scene, choral ensembles faced the cancelation of projects that were years in the making and the possible end to choral singing itself since it was considered dangerous. These artistic directors had to figure out how to keep a professional arts organization relevant and afloat during a shutdown. In these interviews, the conductors discuss their care for the singers, monumental projects—shelved or reimagined, and reimagining the art form.

What were your organization's plans when the COVID-19 pandemic emerged in March 2020?

Craig Hella Johnson: I was going to conduct the Brahms *Requiem* at the Southeastern ACDA [American Choral Directors Association Conference] in Mobile. I was going to fly out on a Monday, and that Friday night on CNN, I probably heard two or three people say, "If you are involved with group gatherings in any way ... If there's any sort of a leadership role or any impact that you have, be responsible and do not engage." So, I mean, you just kind of have to go on a hunch. I'm not a doctor. I'm not a scientist. It was all brand new, but I just heard that conviction in their voice. I just called those wonderful [ACDA] folks and said, "I'm not coming. I don't feel, as a leader, I can stand up and confirm that we should be doing this right now." They were just lovely about it, just incredible.... And then Conspirare, we had just finished a concert series in February, just two weeks before that. We had one other supreme rep, which we had to cancel. That was with Robert Kyr, a piece about global warming and care for the world. We just did that this last May now....

Beth Willer: For Lorelei, it was a very odd situation. We had just done a concert on March 1st and we were taking the rest of the spring off. I was starting a lot of prep on this Julia Wolfe program. We didn't actually lose any gigs in that first 2020 spring, but that had been a planned pause because we were going to have tons of work in the next year. [Laughs] Actually, the day that New York shut down, I was in New York City having a meeting with the entire Julia Wolfe *Her Story* production team and Julia Wolfe. I asked Julia to write this in 2017 with the goal of premiering it in 2020, not only for the 100th anniversary of Women's Suffrage but also for it to align almost perfectly with the 2020 election. We were going to be premiering it in Nashville. I remember talking to a number of the singers and saying, "Well, if this project gets canceled, I'll just weep." We just couldn't believe that the pandemic would go on that long, and we were canceling everything. We had a Tanglewood gig that summer among other things, all canceled.

Joshua Habermann: The thing with Santa Fe [Desert Chorale] is that it works on a festival schedule, so it's not ongoing. We actually got lucky in that we were in an off-season period when the pandemic hit. We usually do a summer festival and a winter festival—it's July, August, December, and then occasionally something else. That year, we had an extra concert in February. We basically just got it in and then, two weeks later, things shut down.

Donald Nally: We [The Crossing] were about to start rehearsals. We were doing Michael Gordon's *Travel Guide to Nicaragua* here in Philadelphia and at Carnegie Hall. We actually postponed for two days to find out what was going to happen. It's interesting because after that piece got canceled, Michael went back and completely rewrote it, and revised it, and came up with something that was a much more meaningful piece, which is really cool. We finally premiered it in the fall, here and at Carnegie Hall. But also, of course, we had a whole *Month of Moderns* planned, three concerts in the summer, a trip to Big Sky, and all that stuff. It all got canceled.

Katherine FitzGibbon: We [Resonance Ensemble] had to pivot in certain ways—just as far as safety and modality, but also in considering the George Floyd protests and the racial justice reckonings. It has been really interesting because we've already been deeply engaged in this work because even who we were before our 2016 mission shift was really relationship-oriented. We have some deep community partnerships that predate even 2016, but certainly that predate 2020. Some of the work we were able to do during the pandemic was built upon things that were already in motion.

We had to postpone Damien Geter's world premiere of *An African American Requiem*. It was huge. It was with the Oregon Symphony in our big downtown concert hall. We commissioned it, and then they jumped on as our partner ... We did it then this past year, in 2022. It was very wonderful. We have this great classical radio station here, All Classical Portland, that is super forward-thinking. They have a recording inclusivity project where they've gotten major funding to record works by both living and dead composers who have historically been underrepresented in classical music radio as well. They immediately decided, "Look, we're going to partner with WQXR New York City and do a live broadcast of the *African American Requiem*." They syndicated the recording and made it available to the entire country so any classical music radio station can play this piece any time they want, for free.

What challenges did your organization have to overcome? How did your focus and plans change to meet those challenges?

Eugene Rogers: EXIGENCE is a project-based choir sponsored by Sphinx. Sphinx as an organization did well financially because people were willing to give money to diversity organizations like they had never done before because of George Floyd and the racial reconciliation that happened in our country....

EXIGENCE had just finished a major performance for the SphinxConnect [Conference] and concerts in Detroit. We only had a few plans, but we wanted to do something in honor of George Floyd and Juneteenth. We learned online a brand-new setting of *Lift Every Voice and Sing*[1] with us bowing to the knee in honor of George Floyd. Anthony McGill began a movement about taking a knee connected to Colin Kaepernick. There were many connections, and *Lift Every Voice and Sing* had an impact we didn't realize. I got more people reaching out to me when it was released.

I had a CD in the hopper that was recorded in December 2019 which is coming out this July. In October, we did our *Glory*[2] for the virtual Gala with Sphinx Virtuosi. That was easier because we already had a recording, so they sang along in their ear to the recording. In October 2021, we had a residency in North Carolina ACDA and did all that with masks. That was our first comeback, and we are back in full force.

Habermann: We did have to deal with the summer festival, which we canceled. We didn't sing through it at all.... We did a fundraising campaign. We realized that if we didn't raise money, we were going to go under. We had to survive so that was what we poured our energy into, and it was really successful. The major push was a sustainability campaign called *Keep Our Voices Singing*. We set our goal for $300,000 and ended up with over $400,000 raised. It was a really big success, and people were generous because the situation was so bad. Everyone was just feeling it like, "Oh, my God, this is terrible, and we'll help."...

We also turned out a lot of recordings. We reached back into the archives, and I listened to every program that we had sung in the previous eight years. We picked out what we liked and then, we shared them with our community of donors. We did a regular Monday thing, *Music Mondays*.

Then I went back, and we actually edited and released a recording of the *Rachmaninov Vespers*[3] that we had done live in 2016.... I've been meaning to go back to it, and honestly, I'm really bad at that of just going back to things that already happened because I'm always more interested in what's coming next. But since there was nothing to do in the present, we went back to the existing material.

And then, in the winter of 2020, we got a quartet of our singers who lived in New York together to do a concert. We rented out a venue, and we filmed them singing with no audience. Then we supplemented that with content from artists all over the country. One of our sopranos who lives in Santa Fe went to the venue where we usually perform, and we shot her singing *Home for the Holidays* by herself in an empty cathedral. We had singers recording for us in their basements.

All of that material we edited into a show called *Home for the Holidays,* and we sold it and/or gave it away as a winter gift. For the closing, we had everybody sing, *Silent Night,* and we picked and chose around two bars for each person singing. I don't think we put them in boxes in the video. There was so much of that that I just didn't want to do it. We did as much live because we felt like that's what our singers are most inspired to do. In truth, they were just glad to be doing anything....

We were worried about our artists—they all sing in different places, and some are freelancers. We took all the contracts and said, "You are automatically all offered for next year. We're going to pre-contract you and we will make a partial prepayment if you want us to ..." It wasn't much, maybe 400 bucks or something, but we offered to advance the money for people who were needing it at that time because their income had dried up overnight.

Socially, we tried to stay connected. We had the Zoom Hangouts. When the *Rachmaninov* came out, we had a launch party on Zoom. Those were as good as it can be within the platform.

Johnson: Just everything got shifted overnight. We were so concerned about just our singers' welfare, of course, with their health, but also just sort of financially taking a hit. We had a few small projects, too, that were going to employ a number of them. They don't earn their whole income with us, of course, but it's not chump change either. They're supporting families. We were in touch with them a lot, "What do you need?" We just made a commitment early on that no matter what was going to happen, we were going to try and support our artists and somehow continue to move forward, finding a way to pay them, even if it wasn't for the work we were planning to do. This organization exists for sounds to come out of them, and they are at the core of who we are.

Just absolutely everything was overturned. We got kind of a bullet list. From an organizational standpoint, we're at a place of saying, "The very thing we do is being identified as a super spreader," and so, sort of our product. I mean, it's just all of a sudden calls into question, "What is it even? Is it even relevant? Is there any aspect to this that needs to move forward?" You even have organizational questions like, "Should we continue to exist?" And then, we focus immediately on just people, like our artists or staff. I think there was this sense of, "How do we keep the fabric of our organization? How do we keep woven together? How do we stay tethered?" It's hard enough when, from an artistic standpoint, we're only together a minimum of four times, maybe seven times a year maximum, and so that's even a job, but then all of a sudden not to be together at all. And this sort of ephemeral thing, this ensemble. We're always trying to emphasize, "This is not just a gig. We're an ensemble." We use that "family" word carefully, but I mean, it's a family of sorts. It's a circle of belonging and all of those things. I think also, from an audience standpoint, [I am] just really aware that this is not a nothing that they experience. They don't just come and kind of hear a little music and clap and go home. This is a real place of belonging for them and a real source of connection to their sort of important life, to the more meaningful life, just connections with music and art in this way and with people.

And then, the morale of these singers ... It's hard enough, the people we employ, the artists we engage. There's enough already. Even though they're talented, they're smart; they got a big ego strength established because they need to be on stage and all of that, but they're still super tender and fragile. [It's] Hard enough to kind of pull all that together as a human being and then get this challenge. You have this psychic weight of what you do is dangerous and could kill people. It's just as heavy a psychological burden, and so, the challenge of that, and then, we decided we're going to make art. If we knew one thing, we're here to create. If there's one thing I know as an artist is that even though limitations can be frustrating, they are what help form and define what we do. And you know this, and I know this: As a creative, give us the more narrow aisle, and we will figure out how to make a skinny piece of art. So, it's like that's a gift....

And then, oh, my Lord in heaven—providing production kits for all these people all over the country with a green screen, a black screen, microphones, and this detailed list of instructions for these dear people. Some of whom are absolutely, "Got it. I'm Susie-one-take," but others need, even the most bright and intelligent of them, hand-holding every step of the way. And then, a phone call during the tears because what's really happening is they're just feeling so alone. I just have one singer in mind whom I love so much. She's in her apartment on her own, and she's just getting her aloneness, sort of the awareness of that amplified as she's struggling with these technical things.

And then, I want to say from the organizational end, the least important but since we're listing challenges, my own sort of morale dip and ... They're dealing with this very same thing and then I'm sitting out after trying to be a container or a world of support for them ... I didn't realize that until like a year in but like, "Wow, I am really hurting." And there's such self-doubt that gets created like, "What is my value? What is my worth?" This is so trivial, but to my soul, it's not. I need to go on but just to say, "Oh, it's real," and asking those same questions. I'm aware that sort of the strange ... part of the strongest things I have to offer in the world are things that are not practical. There's sort of the mystical realm of like, I don't know what it is—if I stand in a certain way and really inhabit my role as a conduit and hold my hands in a certain way, there's something that transmits in that communication that creates a unison, which is not just a practical unison, but it has to do with people really settling and finding each other with shared experience. That's a very holistic thing. That's kind of like as my beautiful mentor says: "That's your medicine. That's your gift to the world." And it's like, "Wow, all of a sudden, my job is going and listening under headphones to every single singer and sort of having to edit, first of all, so that they all line up." It's like cutting, I don't know, carrots or something. It's just layers of practical, layers of financial, layers of psychological and spiritual, and just heaviness. And at the same time, this little spark of grace that says, "We're still here, and to be alive is to create. And so, how do we do that?" ...

[Regarding online programming] I was just like, "Whatever we got, this house is on fire. We got to use whatever we've got to sort of stay connected here." ... I'm not an engineer. I'm not a doctor. I'm not a nurse. What am I? I got a loving heart, and I got music. And it's all we got. And this is as an organization too; we have to stand up with what we have. I never once thought we shouldn't do it. I mean, maybe this is revisionist history what I'm about to say, but I did get too wound up about, "Oh my God, it's not going to sound like Conspirare." Who cares? Who gives a shit when all this is on the line? It's just like I'm going to be so proud to look back and say like, "In the midst of all that, we sang." I mean, proud and grateful. It's been transformational just to our art form, too. And just to kind of shaking off some of that uptightness because I even saw some of the very last holders out of, "[I'm] Never going to do it online. It's not what we do." I was like, "We all got to hold a voice. I'm grateful if that's what you're feeling. You got to hold the voice for right now. That's good because that will provide the overall balance in the long scheme, in the long game." But almost every one of those could have got off that high horse at some point and said, "Oh, yeah, that's right. This house is on fire." I think we just had to move forward.

And then with the online chorale thing, it was just that same questions, "How can we make art? How can we stay connected?" And in a lot of ways, it was also fun. I mean, I learned so much. I don't know if you ever saw the one, which was one of my favorites, I think we called it, *Songs of Unity*.[4] We worked with the South African animation team. That's probably the one I'm most proud of because I got to talk with them about building this dream venue, which was totally made up. It looked like a real place. Everyone said, "Where is that?" But I got to say, "This is what I'd like the venue to be like. I'd like it to be super interior and intimate but also be open to the world." So, with that one, that was the biggest challenge, that particular one, because it was very involved, and we had instruments. That was our first big run with the green screens in a performance kind of way, but I loved it and I loved the message of that because it was really about unity....

In those times, we sensed that we needed to live even closer to our mission, vision, and values—just like cling to it because that's everything. And everything we did needed to be so clear like, "We're doing this because it's mission-driven, period." It's not just some newfangled idea. It's not just a vanity project, not that we would do that anyway necessarily, but it just brings a razor-sharp focus to living our mission. I think for me, a way I did that was to reread. We have a pretty great vision, which I love too, a vision statement, a mission statement, of course, and a value statement. I would reread those regularly. We just talked about what those are together as a staff, particularly with our three-legged stool—me, our managing director, and our board chair, over and over again: "What's our mission? What's our vision? Our values? What's the practical then? Okay. So, with this decision, we have to make what's practical and just try and live that out."

FitzGibbon: As a professional organization, part of equity is making sure you're paying everybody appropriately. It was really important, especially knowing that the jobs for artists during the pandemic [were scarce]. Everybody took a huge and real beating. It was extra important to us that we keep having regular and well-paid opportunities for our people. When we canceled the *African American Requiem* in May 2020, we offered to pay everybody half of what they would have been paid because we had started rehearsals.... We have a couple of really beautiful donors who get what we're doing and were like, "What do you need? I know you're hurting. How can we help make this work?" And then with the CARES (Coronavirus Aid, Relief and Economic Security) funding and other funding, we were able to just be really strategic. But it was incredibly important to us to create opportunities for our artists and to continue to make new art for our audiences safely. We thought, "Okay, this is what we're going to do, and we're going to figure out a way to pay for it." It could have backfired, but as one of the arts mentors here says, "You have to center the artistic and mission goals as your grounding principles, and then you figure out a way. Everything else follows from that" ... and we haven't figured it all out by any means.

We thought, "You know, it's interesting. People are just so used to getting online content for free ..." Since part of our mission is access driven, we wanted to do that. So, we just said, "Okay, look, we're going to just say, 'It's all free. If you could make a donation, pretty please, that would be great.'" Again, sort of like, "I think this will work out." ... What we found was people making lots of small donations, that that just really balloons. And our artists were really grateful to still have these artistic opportunities and experiences during COVID-19.

The other thing was that some of the videos that we put out just had huge numbers of views, like our *Under the Overpass* series.[5] That made us think about, again, if part of your mission is around impact and getting things heard, you can do a concert in Portland, Oregon, and have a few hundred people come to it, or you can put something on YouTube and have a few thousand people....

During the pandemic, we commissioned some new works and recorded them either with socially distanced outdoor sessions or individual studio sessions that we then knit together.... There was a text by Sonya Renee Taylor that she wrote during the pandemic: "We will not go back to normal. Normal never was. Our pre-corona existence was not normal other than we normalized greed, inequity, exhaustion, depletion, extraction, disconnection, confusion, rage, hoarding, hate and lack. We should not long to return my friends. We are being given the opportunity to stitch a new garment. One that fits all of humanity and nature." We got her permission to set it to music and commissioned Jasmine Barnes to write this piece. She wrote this really cool sort of jazz and West African rhythm-inspired a cappella choral setting. That was fun because it felt like we were creating new music that was a reflection of our pandemic experiences and our mission and values: "This is who we are."

And, again, commissioning Jasmine, this amazing young African American female composer who is a superstar.

We were part of the commission and consortium for Mari Esabel Valverde for her work, *We Hold Your Names Sacred.*[6] It was commissioned with the GALA Choirs [Gay and Lesbian Association] and a number of choirs around the country.... And so, we had this video come out in June 2020. We partnered with Pride Northwest, who we work with a lot here, and did both an outdoor thing ... and a video. We did a bunch of research about the women who were being centered in this song. We found pictures of them and learned about their stories. In our video, you see us standing and singing, but also we created this altar with their pictures and candles. And then, because it was designed for online performance, we were able to share a picture of each woman as we said their name with a brief biographical blurb about who they were in the words of their friends or chosen family. That was, again, one of those ways in which doing these virtual things in COVID-19 times ... being able to do this video where you could really bring in the stories, and the photos, and have these ways to reflect what you're singing in a different medium.

We commissioned Damien Geter to write a work that we recorded outdoors. James DePreist was an orchestra conductor, one of Bernstein's proteges, and an African American groundbreaking conductor. He was the Oregon Symphony Music Director for almost 25 years. Somewhere early in the pandemic, we learned that he also had two books of poetry. Damien and I started looking at this poetry. There was this one about how "Even after the shield of your dreams has fallen away, you have an opportunity to rebuild, like a phoenix song." We were like, "Well, isn't that an eminently musically settable and very relatable sort of text right now?" We talked with his widow, who is still living and is here in Portland. She gave us permission to have Damien set it, and we did a video of the commission premiere, too.[7]

Nally: We had to immediately figure out how to keep our community together because The Crossing really is a strong community. The first thing that we did was start a regular meeting where we met every Sunday night at 5:00 for a cocktail hour. We did that for at least six months, just meeting all the time and sharing with each other what was going on in our lives. At the same time, I started this series called *Rising w/ The Crossing*[8] ... Every morning at sunrise, this email would arrive in your inbox, starting in March. It was just a little bit earlier every day because sunrise was just a little bit earlier. It would hit your inbox with a live, past performance. We didn't do canned performances, because we wanted it to be as close to actual live performance as possible. We wanted to be reminded of what it's like when we're together: Singers, audience, friends. I wrote a few paragraphs about why we love that piece, what it was like to do it, and what I hear when I think back about that. There were 60 installments, and then I took a break for June ... And then I came back and did it once a week for the rest of the summer. So, all in all, there were 72 of those. We turned it into an album[9] and it got nominated. Also, it was recognized by the Library of Congress and archived in the National Archives. So that was kind of cool.

Then the other aspect of it was we immediately had to go into a completely different way of thinking about the kind of art that we make in order to give singers work. We really needed to make sure that they had work and had art to make, although we couldn't give them as much ...

One of the first things I did was have major conversations with a couple of our major donors who offered to give us a substantial gift in order to be able to pay out about 85% of all of our commitments to singers through the rest of the season. We did not cancel our contracts with them. We created new work, which we paid for anew because, of course, all of their other work had gone away. That need for new work inspired the development of our *Echoes* amplification kits. They were designed so that each singer was independent and didn't need to be in contact with anyone. They could carry them in their car, carry them to wherever they were going to sing, set them up, put their mic on, turn the amp on, and get their looper and their mixer at their feet ready. And we taught all this on Zoom. We created these new works that, despite living in complete isolation, you could still make a choral piece. The idea behind the design of this was that, even though the singer would be maybe 25 feet away from the listener, the audience is standing in front of or passing by these six-foot pillar speakers; singers could basically be whispering, and it would feel very intimate. In other words, at a great distance, you would hear someone singing very softly and very internally and personally, and you would connect aurally and visually. And then we told stories about what it was like to live at that time. Kevin Vondrak and I wrote this piece called *The Forest*,[10] and we performed it in a forest. It turned out to be very popular, and we remounted it again six months later....

We just had to start over. We couldn't do any of the pieces we'd planned. We had so many commitments to composers to premiere their work. Everything got postponed. We're only now digging ourselves out of that backlog because all of those pieces were designed to be sung in a room where people can stand near and hear each other. Instead, we had to create new pieces. We created this piece with the Warren Miller Performing Arts Center, our usual summer home in Big Sky, that's called *in nature*.[11] It's about 25 minutes. We recorded and filmed each person individually in the icebox in Northern Liberties and projected on the enormous wall behind them a film of the Gallatin River running in Big Sky, which we all know and love. We created a film by editing all those hours and then went to Big Sky, and it was projected on their giant theater screen, with four live singers there that had a very different part in the piece. David Lang wrote this piece for us specifically for this scenario where we would be here in Philadelphia and they would be there in Big Sky, but we would be singing together. We would connect ... again, across the distances of our isolation.

I wasn't interested in a Zoom choir—that kept a number of communities together. I couldn't really watch them because I was experiencing such isolation myself. I was fortunate enough that my husband and I could navigate this together, whereas so many of my singers didn't have that, and so they were really, really isolated and alone. I wanted to make pieces that were about isolation and aloneness, and to embrace that time. I felt like Zoom choirs didn't really do that; they kind of tried to do the opposite of that.

Funding was a tremendous challenge, but we weathered that really quite well, because the government did help to look after people, and our donors were very generous and very consistent with their generosity during the pandemic. It was stressful, but that part of it actually worked out okay. And then, of course, there's just creating; going for long, long walks and coming back and going, "Okay, I know what we're doing for Christmas. We're going to make this film. I'm going to write the score. It's going to be pretty raw, but that's how I'm feeling, so I'm just going to make a piece about that." So that's *You can Plan on Me*.[12] That's the film where they're putting all these photographs—of all the singers as children at Christmas—into this photograph book, and the score is being sung behind it.

Some of that creativity steered us to film. And in those films, whether they were made in a huge field standing in a 230-foot diameter circle or a barn, the feeling of separation is always present; the reality of not being able to touch. We also made animated films. Among the most poignant of those is *protect yourself from infection*.[13] By an amazing coincidence, we collaborated with David Lang a year before that to record individual lines and a list of the deceased in Philadelphia during the 1918 pandemic. The original was for a parade, but NPR's *Performance Today* invited us to make a piece of it, so we did that in an animated film with art by our tenor, Steven Bradshaw, and direction by our friend, Brett Snodgrass. The result is strangely eerie and moving. We also made films about immigration and homelessness.

And some of that creativity resulted in *Carol's after a Plague*,[14] which was kind of our culminating pandemic thing a year later at Christmas of 2021. We did these 12 pieces by 12 composers; their personal response to, "What is a carol? What is a plague?" And that plague might be poverty, or … We have all these plagues that we live with all the time. We just live with them. We live with the plague of gun violence, wealth distribution, bigotry, and racism. It's only when people who are in control can see the damage that you're going to find a solution to that problem. We're the fortunate recipients of the fact that the pandemic hit all communities. It didn't discriminate against communities, so we solved that problem. I'm convinced we have the ability to solve all of those other problems, but we just choose not to do it. And so, we make pieces about them. The 12 works are incredibly different; many address grief or race issues, and they are threaded together by Shara Nova's carols in which she attempts to grapple with the trauma of guilt and her own whiteness.

Willer: Gradually, everything just fell off for the next year we had planned. We were going to be at the National Gallery. We were going to be at Eastman and Duke. We had some non-Wolfe tours, but we also had performances with five symphonies that were all just one-at-a-time canceled. It was just a slow realization. I definitely went through a period of panic. I remember a board meeting where I was just completely resistant to the idea of doing anything virtual, and we just needed to wait for this to be over. And in the meantime, I'm just going to plan for these projects we've already been planning on.

Unlike a lot of pro groups, I'm thinking of these groups that have a million or more in their budgets, Lorelei doesn't have the necessary cash flow if we're not touring. That's our primary income. We pay our singers well and so the idea of starting anything new—I mean I would've loved to just commission a bunch of new works that were intended for virtual performance, but I couldn't make that happen. And so, what I ended up deciding to do was to do a bunch of smaller virtual projects that anticipated the things we would be doing once we were back to normal. The *Wolfe* was something that we talked about like hologram performances. We'd be offstage but [Laughs] all these conversations were like, "How could we make it work?" because some of the orchestras didn't cancel until well into the fall of 2020. And so, we were like, "Well, is there a way we could do it?" Eventually, we stopped trying to figure out how to do that in any altered way because it was the premiere. And the good news is voting rights don't get any less relevant going into 2022 and 2023. So, that piece, she had more time to write it and to respond to the current situation, and that kind of evolved behind the scenes.

We had been planning to and had good funding for a new commission of Christopher Cerrone, a piece setting the Beaufort Scale,[15] a 19th century wind scale, with visual projections by Hannah Wasileski. It was intended to be this sort of multimedia presentation anyway. We commissioned and recorded the first movement of that at home in our living rooms with our not amazing microphones. Hannah did the visuals and we worked with the engineer that we intended to work with. The awesomeness of that project for me was recognizing what could be done with a multitrack recording and all of the filtering and ways that we could incorporate electronics and use stereo sound. We did some experimentation with these Bose spatialized-audio headphones that you could move your head, and it would change where you were hearing different tracks. I kind of had this mind explosion moment of "Wow, we should do this sometimes regardless of the pandemic." There are things we can do with a recording of a piece that we just can't do in a live acoustic setting. It just completely changed my idea of what we could do.

The other project that was sort of in the works was we had just released our David Lang *love fail*[16] album in June 2020 right after the pandemic hit. We had planned to tour that with a dance quartet from Pilobolus. We were commissioning all this new choreography from Renee Jaworski and they managed to get their dancers together. They did the bubble and stuff. They recorded the dance of two movements of *love fail*[17] with our recording. They are these really beautifully produced videos that are sort of a preview of this project that we're still planning. The *Cerrone* is just going to happen. We're going to just workshop it this spring and premiere it next fall. All this stuff is still in the works, but these ended up being sort of marking pieces that were things we were going to pay for anyway. We were going to pay to commission the *Cerrone*. We were going to pay to commission this choreography, and it was really just a matter of the recording and the editing.

We did do one performance that I had not planned on. We decided to do a Christmas video[18] where we stood 12 feet apart at a beautiful hall in Rockport, Mass. I think I did it with only six singers because that was all I could fit on that stage with the necessary distancing. We went through a number of precautions so that we could sing unmasked in the recording. We did a ridiculously long recording day. It was like the program we used to do at the Met Museum for Christmas. It was rep that we loved and felt really special to come back to, and that for many of us, I think, was the first time we had sung in person with anyone. We recorded it in October of 2020, and I remember I hadn't conducted for months and waved my arms. We were doing this Renaissance motet, and it was totally new to us, and I had made the addition. I had some ideas, and I was like, "Can I just lead you through this bit?" It felt so good to just raise something and have people respond. I remember that very well, that little moment of rehearsal....

The other thing that was totally new was that we started doing some educational things. We did some multitracking multi-session workshops with Princeton Girl Choir and Philadelphia Girl Choir. We did some live sessions focused on technique and body awareness. And then for multi-tracking, we used SoundTrap. We helped them record and coached them on repertoire. That was really fun. It was a steep learning curve. I couldn't do it because I was teaching eight hours a day, five days a week at Peabody [Institute] ... I was using SoundTrap every day, so I was really comfortable with it, but I had to train Lorelei to use SoundTrap. It was kind of an amazing platform because it was pretty quick to learn. The kids could really do it themselves, but I had learned there was a certain way to do it and make them successful by creating all these guide tracks. So, that was fun, and I think something that we could continue to do, virtual education work, I mean. I think we connected with more young people in that area than we would in a typical year, and I know we did more than that. We did a lot of Q&As with college groups and even some high school groups where we just talked about our careers and how we're dealing with the pandemic, and that was also very fruitful.

Now it's been this slow build back into touring, which has not been as fast as anyone would like it to be. Everything got delayed two years instead of one, so now most of the *Wolfe* is happening this year (2022–2023), and the National Symphony is delayed until 2025. Last year, we did do a live tour in the spring, that was our first self-produced concert. We didn't do anything in the fall, which part of me felt like we should have done but then with all the variants, it ended up being the right choice. And then what we did actually in the summer and the fall when we weren't doing any live performance, we did a lot of recording. We recorded James Kallembach's

Antigone.[19] We recorded Jessica Meyers' *i long and seek after*,[20] which are Sappho settings. We finally recorded Scott Ordway's *North Woods*, which we commissioned in 2014 and never got a good recording of. So, those are all EPs. The *Meyer*'s almost ready, and the *Meyer* was one that I recorded in a studio. We did some multitracking because it's one of these pieces that you can do something with that you couldn't do in a live performance because it's got a lot of belting. We're doing some old radio filters and stuff that I just would've never thought to do. I think honestly to me, it's given new life to that piece, whereas the *Kallembach* and *Ordway*, we recorded totally traditionally at Mechanics Hall, which was also a dream to record there. That was my first unmasked, un-distanced thing in summer 2021....

In spring 2019, we had just finished a new strategic plan. It was all about shifting our income model because we have, as a touring organization at this point, 70% of our income is earned and 30% is contributed. That's a problem when a pandemic comes because there goes 70% of your income. And prior to knowing this pandemic was coming, [we] said, "This doesn't seem really sustainable. We should probably switch to at least like a 60/40." We're probably not going to get to 50/50. Self-producing organizations tend to be a lot more contributed but we're paying pro musicians, and you just can't make that much money in ticket sales. It's a losing game, so we had started to make that shift and, of course, we had made all these goals of increasing our staff during this time. By summer 2021, we were going to create a full-time development position. We were going to move our executive director to full-time, but we had planned for this huge staff expansion ... I don't want to say none of that has happened, but it's been happening more slowly than we would have liked. We have put some energy, with the help of an expert and generous board member, into expanding our contributed income.

The other thing that was absolutely essential, were all of these government, state and national level grants and PPE grants, etc. that supported organizational needs. That's how we recorded. We would have never been able to do those recording projects without that. I had to convince the board that, "Yes, we've lost operating funds but the people who really lost money are our artists. Rather than just throwing the money for work they didn't get to do back into organizational expenses, let's create a project and pay them right now and let's get something out of it that's useful for us." Recordings, they don't make money, right? They only spend money, but they are essential, especially now and during this pandemic and in the way that they preview our work but also archive our work for future audiences. I was able to convince them to spend a large amount of that on artistic contracts, something that allowed us to have that continuity. The challenge for the ensemble was we just didn't see each other nearly as much as we would have, and just long periods of time between when we'd be in a room together. That was hard and we already had some new artists coming in and some artists going out. We were already in this period of transition right before the pandemic of expanding our roster, so that was hard. Ultimately, I think it's given us some new energy. You just kind of get in a rhythm, and you function a certain way. You make a certain sound, and now when we get together, I feel like there's different energy, which is good.

How did you keep hope alive in your choir? What did you do to help your singers cope with not being able to sing? How did you meet the needs of your singers?

Nally: I think it's important, right from the beginning, to know that you can't meet the needs of the singers. That's a starting point to understand that we were a box of broken toys before the pandemic (What the fuck were we when the pandemic came?) and to use that as a jumping off point for trying to be strong and to make difficult decisions. Luckily, we have an amazing team here. Kevin—our assistant conductor, and also our artistic associate and coordinator of all things, and one of my closest friends and someone who I trust with everything about these people—he and I spoke quite thoughtfully a lot of times about what direction to go, and to embrace that there was all this emotion and just no place to put it. The emotional side of it, it isn't possible or even appropriate for someone in my position to try to manage that, but to at least acknowledge it in the room and keep it in the room was challenging, but for me, I think, necessary, and I think for our group, too.

Johnson: I think just practical stuff to just staying in touch, emails, and phone calls. We had monthly Zoom sessions for several months where all the singers could just come and say, "Hi." I said two- or three-minutes' worth of, "We love you. We're here with you," but then just opened it up. People would share sad stories, or they would share jokes. They loved it. Then, one-on-one conversations, too. I think a big thing was just paying them, and it was really expensive. Anything we canceled, we paid. We paid them their contracts, and that was really hard to do because we had to hustle. We had to ask donors, "Will you please pay for no end result here but just people? It's an investment in people." I think that meant a lot in a way that was almost the first and most important thing because it's sort of sometimes like "thoughts and prayers." In this age of gun violence like, "That's really important and meaningful, but actually, just can we do something practical to stop this?" I think with that, just receiving a check and a card that says, "We love and appreciate you." …

And then the practical stuff of these production kits we did that were really packed with practical helps. The instructions were really carefully detailed. We thought, "Who amongst our people are visual learners? Who are oral learners? Who are experiential?" We would just say, "If you want a private connection, call me or one of the production team. If you want bit by bit detailed written instructions, here you go." Then, we would do a Zoom presentation walking people through every step and Q&A sessions.…

It was a great opportunity to really emphasize the value of people themselves even more than normal.… and then, actually, I will say, allow ourselves to be nourished and refreshed by that mission and vision. I went back to it not just for directives but also for renewal. When you're tired, it's like, "Why are we doing this? Oh, yeah, that's right. This is what we said. This is what we said we were, who we were, and what we want to inhabit in this life."

Is there anything you did or learned during the pandemic that you would keep post-pandemic?

FitzGibbon: If you're trying to change the world [Laugh] (we hope), then having that opportunity to have that kind of [online] platform [is worth keeping]. And then, again, figuring out a way to pay for it. I feel like that is very much on mission for us. It was a really good learning experience to realize that

that was a way to reach more people and a different way to invest. Our budgets, since then, have had more budget allotted for video creation and online content, and making sure that continues to be a piece of what we do. At the least, we're posting our concerts online afterward, so that's been a change, too.

Habermann: First, we learned that we need to video record everything we do. Also, we learned how much people love our organization and how kind people are when you're in distress because that was existential for us, for sure. The universities and big institutions weren't going anywhere, but small nonprofits like ours could easily go under. Trying to support overhead without income was a real crisis. In the end, our community stepped up big time to support us and see us through.

Johnson: Kind of everything. Yeah, I don't want to throw any of those skill sets out. I got to personally learn some new Logic and Pro Tools kind of skills, which I'm no expert but, that was great for me. I was delighted [with the] kind of new editing ears I gained. We, as an organization, brought on new collaborators, I mean, wonderful new partners that we would not have met without this time, and we want to keep connected. We really built an audience of new friends around the world. We regularly hear from them, "Please, keep streaming because we don't want to lose that." If we don't stream a concert, we hear about it from many people. We can't afford to do it all the time because it's a real thing, but we love that. I mean, the thousands of people that we got to meet through the pandemic that we would not have known otherwise. And then, just in general, our production values were enhanced, that we've kind of upped our game in those ways. We want to keep bringing those visual elements when they're appropriate, when they seem relevant to our performances.

Willer: Definitely, [I would keep] this idea of different methods of recording. It's an absolute art to do just straight acoustic recording. I think that will always be our specialty but that was exciting to me to learn about the incredible things that can be done in post [production]. And then first of all, all of our board meetings are virtual now, which has allowed us to expand to having more people from other parts of the country…. And then, as far as the artistic work goes, nobody wants to rehearse online but you can coach language really well online. I had a group doing some *Janacek* at Tanglewood this summer. We got a Hungarian coach, and they

	were able to coach months in advance. It was awesome. I'll never do language coaching any other way because then you can set up one-on-one meetings for people, and they can do it when it's convenient for them.
Nally:	*Echoes*,[21] we really enjoyed them. We enjoyed singing outside, and it's a way for us to go outside and do some singing, amplified with stuff we already own, and we don't have to reinvent the wheel. We also created pieces for installations on them so that they could live in real time without people. We created unsynchronized pieces, like Paul Fowler's *Obligations*,[22] on a really fantastic poem by a Lakota poet, Layli Long Soldier; that, too, is designed to also be an installation. I think we learned about some of our priorities; what's important about presentation, and what we *thought* was but isn't. And then, I, personally, went through a lot of soul searching and decided to leave my college position.

How did the COVID-19 pandemic affect your programming?

Habermann:	I tossed out the programming and started over. It usually gets done two years in advance, but I ended up redoing it three times because the circumstances were changing from month to month. In the end, we were able to pull off a summer season in 2021 and have been going strong ever since.
Johnson:	Everything costs more now because we used to have singers in host homes. Singers generally really were enjoying that, but we've had to be in single room hotels now. All of our costs have doubled, and it's insane. We're doing, at the moment, less. The same amount just costs twice as much. So, that's a bummer but we have really rallied to try and meet that with intensified fundraising, etc.
Rogers:	Not really. Racial reconciliation wasn't for me. It's for other people. I always have been programming things that deal with BIPOC people. I'm not doing anything differently, except now more people want it.
FitzGibbon:	We'd been budgeting for one commission a year on average. Then we realized, "Well, we could do a few things. People are interested in supporting it. I think we can make this work financially, fingers crossed." But it has meant though we've been doing more commissioning—on average, a commission per concert … So, a cool thing that's changed is our commitment to new repertoire, like, "Commissioning is the best. Let's do as much of it as we can."

Is there anything else you would like to say about singing during the pandemic?

Rogers: Back in the day, people would say, "I want to go to this school, study with this teacher. I'll pay the 50 grand a year." At U of M, we don't have as many as we used to have singing in the choirs, majoring in voice. People are not willing to do it if you're not going to give them scholarship money ... That's partly COVID-19. That's partly the economy. However, on the community side, people are hungry again. They want to be a part of an engaged, active community. For me, it's interesting to see where it's going to affect the professional side of things. Will we have as many people to draw from professionally for the art form?

Nally: I always knew that we have an amazing community of artists in our midst, but the experience of going through the pandemic with them and having them go, "I'm going to do whatever you guys want to do. I just want to sing with my friends. So if you ask me to carry a frickin' backpack and an over-the-shoulder amplification kit and deal with hot and cold and rain and bugs, I'm going to do that ..." I felt like we were doing these things, and our community really believed in my crazy ideas; not that they questioned them at other times, but there was just this energy of *"Make it happen."* So that's something that we should be really careful to not let go.

Notes

1. EXIGENCE, *Lift Every Voice and Sing*, https://youtu.be/rs3XxV5M7i8
2. EXIGENCE, *Glory*, https://youtu.be/37Bq5T_lV1c
3. Santa Fe Desert Chorale, *Rachmaninov All-Night Vigil*, https://youtube.com/playlist?list=OLAK5uy_m03cSSM4XWbfnAYl9Mn38Tm0YvL7Vb2U0
4. Conspirare, *Unity: Songs of Invitation*, https://youtu.be/y_XE3_vD5LQ
5. Resonance Ensemble, *Under the Overpass*, https://www.resonancechoral.org/under-the-overpass
6. Resonance Ensemble, *We Hold Your Names Sacred,* https://youtu.be/-LBDVipDOIE
7. Resonance Ensemble, *After Time Has Gnawed Away the Shield of Dreams*, https://www.youtube.com/watch?v=-d9hFMTEqDE
8. The Crossing, *Rising w/ The Crossing*, https://www.projects.crossingchoir.org/rising
9. The Crossing, *Rising w/ The Crossing* (Live), https://music.youtube.com/playlist?list=OLAK5uy_mD-iIjFY3ocromenqIXWcNnFu4R4SGXTo&
10. The Crossing, *The Forest – A Film by the Crossing*, https://youtu.be/sJgok21MXM0
11. The Crossing with Roots in the Sky, *in nature*, https://www.projects.crossingchoir.org/nature
12. The Crossing, *You can Plan on Me*, https://www.projects.crossingchoir.org/christmas-2020
13. The Crossing, *protect yourself from infection*, https://www.projects.crossingchoir.org/protect-yourself-from-infection

14 The Crossing, *Carols after a Plague*, https://www.projects.crossingchoir.org/carols
15 Lorelei Ensemble, *Beufort Scales*, https://www.loreleiensemble.com/look-up
16 Lorelei Ensemble, *love fail*, https://www.loreleiensemble.com/all-albums/love-fail
17 Lorelei Ensemble, *love fail*, https://www.loreleiensemble.com/love-fail
18 Lorelei Ensemble, *Jul, Jul Strålande Jul*, https://youtu.be/4QjWQb4jiEw
19 Lorelei Ensemble, *Antigone*, https://www.loreleiensemble.com/all-albums/antigone
20 Lorelie Ensemble, *i long and seek after*, https://www.loreleiensemble.com/meyer-i-long-and-seek-after
21 The Crossing, *Echoes*, https://www.projects.crossingchoir.org/echoes
22 The Crossing, *Obligations*, https://www.projects.crossingchoir.org/obligations

6 New Choirs
Inspired to Create

Interviewees

Martín Benvenuto, Artistic Director and Founder, 21V
Jason Max Ferdinand, Artistic Director and Founder, Jason Max Ferdinand Singers

Introduction

In June 2019, Chorus America sponsored a professional chorus incubator, and many more participants showed up than anticipated. The concept of starting a new choir was on many people's minds, and they were eager to learn about the process. A monumental amount of work and time is required to assemble a new artistic endeavor, and finding funding for a professional chorus is even more challenging in the best of times. While most choruses slowed or shut down during the COVID-19 pandemic, some choirs were born amidst the pandemic restrictions. This chapter focuses on two conductors inspired to create new professional ensembles despite the pandemic limitations. They both share their visions of how their unique choruses can create a more inclusive world through song. The birth of these choirs demonstrates that when all seems lost, there will be people who dare to create something beautiful.

Did you plan to launch your choir during the pandemic? How did you bring about a new organization during the pandemic?

Martín Benvenuto: No, I really didn't have an implementation plan that I changed, but rather the challenge was, "Well, now we have all these things thought out: We have audition materials. We have values that we vetted through focus groups. We have this basic marketing structure, and we're ready to say that we want to make an appearance in the world. But do we wait

DOI: 10.4324/9781003330486-7

until we can sing in a mask?" To be honest, in June of last year [2021], I was thinking, "I don't know that I want to start unless we can sing freely. Do I really want to do masked singing?" This constant change really pushed us to make decisions. I'm not sure that that was the right decision, to be honest. I'm sure it's different for each one of us, but change created a sense of urgency in us conductors, and at the same time, we could just be a little bit in our heads for a long time. What came to the top was keeping our art form alive so that humans could have this experience and share it with others in some way. So that clearly rose to the top. Then, the ways that we did that were less than ideal, but we all understood, at some level, that that was preeminent....

The first "performance" was at the Redwood Grove in Berkeley, at the UC [University of California] Berkeley Botanical Gardens. It was a recording session. That's when we released a pre-premiere of our first commission *Praise Song for Tulsa*.[1] So, at that time, I was pretty sure that I could get singers to come together and feel reasonably comfortable, if we produced the recording with a set of protocols with which people felt okay. So that's how we got to that decision, "Let's do this. It'll be a teaser for, hopefully, the first concert in-person [concert], in April, which is what happened."

One of the things that I think is hopefully unique about this group is this idea of bringing a virtual component into part of the programming. I don't know how long this will sustain itself in our art form in general and/or in 21V. It's a stereotypical example of making lemonade out of lemon here, "Let's use this to actually go further in our reach. This is something now we're all used to. Why not involve more people that would embrace this project if they were local?" It was clear to me that virtual components added to live performances were going to have a lasting effect because we were so quickly changing our focus. At the beginning, I felt that "Well, maybe if the group starts, and we can't sing without masks, maybe we'll start with virtual projects." But then, as time went on, the possibility of in-person became more tangible, even if outdoors. Then that shifted. Now we have this new thirst for developing something that's worth presenting in the virtual space. I think that it's intimidating and at the same time exciting.

Jason Max Ferdinand: No, absolutely not. My plan was to lay low and get through to the end of it [pandemic]. As I was sharing, [a new choir was started because of the ask of Voces8 [regarding an Aeolians Christmas virtual choir release] and, more specifically, [Voces8 manager] Robin Tyson. He just encouraged me to think about it. If we did it, it would be launched in the Voces8 virtual music series platform. So, we did that [Aeolians Christmas virtual choir release], and then Voces8 asked me if I wanted the Aeolians to be part of the spring festival since that one went so well. The timelines were just so tricky because they needed a video by February, and school started in the middle of January. So, I said, "No, absolutely not." Then Robin said, "Well, have you considered starting a professional group?" And I was like, "No, why would I do that now?" He said, "Well, you might want to think about it." So, again, that's how we started. I just called up people. We met sometime in February, I think, and recorded the video and the audio and sent it off. And that was the beginning....

Honestly, the initial thought was just to get that first recording done. Because it started so suddenly, I had no long-term plans. It was just to get the Voces8 project[2] done. Then we were like, "Let's just see what happens," because the reality was that it was either going to be really, really bad, or it could turn into something. So, we had six weeks from when I said "yes" to do it. Six weeks to get the video to Voces8. So, I started calling people and started choosing repertoire at the same time. In retrospect, it was crazy, just trying to put it together. I still don't really know how we did it because there was no kind of dedicated rehearsal time. The rehearsals were the recordings....

I've always had a sound in my head. My college-age choir, the Aeolians had a certain sound, but I always knew there was ... Every age group you can do certain things. So, if I did have a professional choir, I always had a soundscape idea in my mind of what I wanted it to sound like. The people that I picked represent what I was hearing, which is a sound that translates well to all styles, and which is really centered from the bass up ... That's why I have Angelo Johnson in the group. He and that type of voice is where it starts for me. If you looked at where he stood in the group, he's dead in the middle because it reverberates from the center. So, that's the basis of the sound.... Angelo has consistently reminded me of that [starting a professional choir] for all these years. So, when this project came, I think he was probably one of the first people I called. And he started, just like he did for 20 years before [for the master's recital], started calling some names and putting things together. He's been a constant [Laughs] when it comes to this. So, yeah, he's in heaven right now.

At the time, I was still in Huntsville, so we all met in Maryland at a church there and recorded all the audio over two days. Then we spent some time on the visual part of it on day three, but it was, "Rehearse, all right, hit record. Let's go." We pieced everything together with masks on and the whole nine [yards]. We had people who even got sick the night before ... One member of the group you may know, Cindy Ellis, she came up and she was sight-reading everything because Andrea Williams got COVID-19 like right before. We flew Cindy up the night before from Miami and she read the whole show. She's in the group now because of that. She's really, really good. So, it was just rehearse, phrase, record, rehearse, phrase, record. That's how we did it.

What challenges did you have to overcome to establish your new ensemble?

Ferdinand: Literally the challenge of not being able to rehearse and our recording had literally pieces of phrases together. We had an incredible engineer, Paul Vasquez. He especially, more than me, was under pressure. After a long day, he would have to go to his hotel room and piece it together because then the last part of the project was a visual part. So, he was up half the night, and I would be up, too, because I'm waiting on him to approve edits. [Paul would say,] "Okay, Jason, is this enough space between this fermata? Is this the right take?" It was just loopy for like three days. So, the challenge of putting it together was literally the challenge of doing everything so quickly because we needed it done fast.

Benvenuto: Well, from a practical standpoint, rehearsal and performance venues were and continue to be in flux. One of the things that when we decided that we were going to start was that we were going to go in the continuum from safe, safer, to safest. We were going to stay on the safest side. So that meant that in the fall of 2021 we did everything outdoors. The weather can get a little tricky in the Bay Area. That was very stressful. For our second rehearsal, we had a rainstorm forecast. We rehearsed in the church in their memorial garden outside and were borrowing lighting equipment from another choir that had been rehearsing there. The day of contingency plans included: "How do we unplug these things without electrocuting ourselves if we start to rehearse?" It was scary. Then the third rehearsal was at my house on my patio. My partner built me a little six-foot piece of wood stick that I used to measure the required six feet. I spent one Saturday afternoon playing around with the stick to see if I could actually fit 19 chairs on the patio, and I could barely....

Regarding implementation, auditioning singers on Zoom, yeah, not ideal, but you make it work.... But the gathering of people in a physical space, that was a big deal. Many rehearsal venues that I had used before were saying, "Well, we're not taking any new groups," or "We're taking a break," or "We decided to refurbish the sanctuary." People were really using the pandemic to reevaluate what they were doing.

One of the decisions to make was where the choir would be based. Is it an Oakland choir? A San Francisco choir? Is this an East Bay choir? I didn't want to limit it geographically, so we had an equitable compromise. Once the roster was finalized, I chose venues according to travel time and distance—so different sets of COVID-19 regulations, different contracts, different certificates of insurance.

How did you find the strength, creativity, and resilience to start something new amid the COVID-19 pandemic?

Ferdinand: Everybody had a different approach during COVID-19, what their mindset was going to be coming out of COVID-19. I used COVID-19 as a time to really try and replenish energy and replenish thoughts. I was always saying, "Guys, let's work on skill sets and whatever we can learn during the pandemic." I contemplated the fact that it would be an atrocity to do things the way we did it before the pandemic. I was really just trying to better myself, whether it was music or just in general, just trying to grow. But when we did come together, the group members were so excited to be doing something during the pandemic. For a lot of them, especially those that were in music, nothing was musically happening. There were no gigs. There were no church choirs. There was nothing happening. So, they were very, very excited to do it. All of us I think were a little tentative, "Oh my gosh, are we going to get sick?" You just never knew what was going to happen, but they approached it with positivity. They were even happier when we heard some of the final product, like, "Oh my gosh, this is what we did with masks on and under such strict testing …" We could still create something that was beautiful that hopefully lasts for a long time.

Benvenuto: It was hard. I think to an extent, me sharing my ideas excited some people that they knowingly or unknowingly were pressuring and encouraging me to keep going. I think that the central inspiration for me to start this group was the idea of inclusivity and being a player of this moment we're in, a movement toward a new level of embracing communities that have been left behind. I feel strongly about being a part of this movement away from "acceptance," away from "tolerance," and more toward embracing and actively engaging with people who have unique life experiences.[3] We are enriched by learning through all of these different areas that 21V is trying to cover. So, I felt an urgency, a sense that the moment was ripe for a group like ours.

What kept you going during the pandemic?

Ferdinand: It was the project. It was family. For my household, it was great being home for a long stretch and not having to be on the road. That was a beautiful thing.… COVID-19 had a lot of blessings in it, a lot of blessings. COVID-19 also gave us a chance to reach so many corners of the world. We're talking to people in New Zealand over Zoom—classrooms in all time zones. It came to a point where I just had to shut it [guest speaking] down for a period. I think when I got to May, I was like, "All right, I'm not doing anymore" because I was in people's classrooms at six AM my time. But it was great and normally that wouldn't ever happen. You'd be in an eighth-grade class in Kentucky or some class up in Boston. It was great because people had more access to whoever. So, there were great things that came out of COVID-19 I think, but so many people also didn't make it through COVID-19.

There was one thing we did in the early days of COVID-19. There was a lady in an organization, right around the Washington Monument. They planted all these little white flags and at the time, the death toll was around 700,000, I think. I don't remember how, but they asked us to sing for that. It was right near the new African American Museum, and the monument was right there, and all the flags. They had a counter, a real-life electronic counter. So, you would literally be in the program and see the counter clicking up. I'm like, "Oh, man, this is so real." A lot of people didn't make it. I think all of us were affected by COVID-19 in some way and knew somebody. I guess it's made us more human, you know. It's made us more human....

Did the COVID-19 pandemic affect your programming?

Benvenuto: Yes, definitely. It has affected it and inspired it at the same time. We opened our inaugural *Beyond Binary* concert[4] with Stephen Paulus's *Kin to Sorrow*, setting an Edna St. Vincent Millay poem. "Am I kin to sorrow? Am I just trying to embrace sorrow?" The poem personifies sorrow in a way that, in the end, the poet says, "Oh, come in. Come in sorrow." It just invites it in as a way to destroy the "enemy" of sorrow by accepting it. I feel that our choral community has been so focused on how we move forward and that we could have acknowledged more fully the loss and its ripple effects on so many people around the world.

Ferdinand: Some of it was driven by the pandemic, like the spiritual *Nobody Knows the Trouble I've Seen*[5] for sure.... Some of it was to honor some of our mentors from our past, so we did a setting of Psalm 1,[6] which was written by Nathan Carter. It was very romantic. He was trying to pay homage to Brahms when he wrote it. Then we wanted to add a twist to it, so we had John, our pianist and orchestrator—he just wrote an entirely new accompaniment so you could sing the original choir parts to the new accompanying treatment. We did that in a couple of cases. We did that with the old setting *The Holy City*.[7] John said, "You know, Jason, I really want to give this a more contemporary treatment." He just changed the entire accompaniment, but we could still sing the original setting. Then we had some songs of hope in there, like the spiritual *Didn't It Rain*.[8] We did a setting of *Oh, Praise the Lord* by Adolphus Hailstork[9] to try again to pay homage to an African American composer, but writing something other than a spiritual. We did some pieces by people in the group, Cedric Dent.[10] I think we did one of my pieces. It was a mixed bag of rep.

Themes for me kind of come in spurts. It comes slowly, but definitely I think we want to involve audiences more. That could take on so many different ways. Whether that means we do more pre-concert talks or we stay back after and talk to people or we program things that are a little more [participatory] ... Like, for example, the concert we did here [at Syracuse University] with the last song, *Human Heart*.[11] I don't think we would have done that as readily before COVID-19, but people resonate with that type of stuff way more now than they did then. So, finding those moments that you could involve the audience and let them feel a part of the process is key now, I think.... We didn't do this song on Sunday [at Syracuse University], but we did it for ACDA [National Conference] *Safe in His Arms*[12] about a kid feeling safe in his parents' arms or some authority figure. I wrote that with my wife, but a lot of times we link that to what's going on in the Ukraine.... So, when you perform songs like *Safe in His Arms* or something like that, the audience all of a sudden is like, "Oh my gosh, this is a real circumstance that's happening with fellow human beings." Still yes, singing all the classic stuff is good. And hopefully, those things people see in a new light, like we did [with] Handel's *Sing Unto God* with that new text.... This new text just brings so much hope, and it's in modern-day English and ... You can relate to it more.... So, just little things like that that our audience can resonate with—same old music but new text. I think the choral field needs more intentionality now as we get out of COVID-19 or post-COVID-19 ... whatever you call this new season.

Is there anything you did or learned during the pandemic that you would keep post-pandemic?

Ferdinand: We're singing in all these different spaces. You just have to be malleable. It's never all going to be the same. I think the pandemic really kind of taught us that.... It's taught me that you have to embrace challenges and try to learn all you can through them, because in the long run it makes us better. Just try to approach it with that sense of being positive, a sense of curiosity, and optimism and just try to learn more about people. Empathy, curiosity, empathy, and optimism— I think if people approach all their challenges like that, we would be better off for it. And I get it, some people gave up during COVID-19 and that's human nature. I'm not mad at them or anything, but we have to change our mindsets to get through any sort of challenge.

We have an internal joke about that in the group. I felt like we were flying the plane and building it all at the same time. Most groups start with structure behind it—funding, your board, and then you start performing. We did the opposite where we performed, and then it was, "Okay, what do we do now? So, what did we see?" It was funny because just yesterday when I had that five o'clock meeting, it was with my planning team and Robin Tyson from Voces8 just to try and figure out what next steps should be for us. Cedric Dent was on that call, as well, because he's been through all of that with Take 6. We want to be in it for the long haul because we feel now we have something unique to offer and something to say. We just need people and processes around to help do that and that's the short answer. I could say so much more on that.

I guess you never know, but I don't think this group will be full-time to the point that is all the singers do. For us, I think our formula is going to be doing concerts on Friday nights, depending on where it is and whether can we get there in time on Friday nights, Saturday, and early concert Sunday afternoon. Then everybody must get home. So, that for us would be the model, I think. We also have an educational component attached that we've been doing in schools— elementary and high schools that we'll continue to do. So, that's where we're sitting right now. And then trying to develop a lot more of the recording arm, whether that means trying to get a big label or a small label and how all of that

	looks. So, really, we're still building the plane and just trying to make sure we have the right people around us who have been there, done that, and just kind of see how it all ends up.
Benvenuto:	Artists now more than ever are telling stories of our time. We have such an opportunity to follow the trajectory of an issue, or of a person, or of an activist, or of an artist, and be more specific and dig deeper. It is interesting to think about how we communicate verbally when we speak about our art now. There's an urgent need to engage in a concise manner: Trying to capture a piece in a sentence or a composer in a paragraph is almost futile, but also necessary.

Notes

1. 21V, *Praise Song for Tulsa*, https://youtu.be/NE4QP5Nvgug
2. Jason Max Ferdinand Singers, *Live from London Spring Highlights – New Beginnings*, https://youtu.be/_Lpi_WusRJA
3. 21V, *The Making of 21V*, https://youtu.be/KposW2lZqG8
4. 21V, *Beyond the Binary*, https://www.21vchoir.org/beyondbinary
5. Jason Max Ferdinand Singers, *Nobody Knows the Trouble I've Seen*, https://youtu.be/ra5Jm25A9Vw
6. Jason Max Ferdinand Singers, *Psalm 1*, https://youtu.be/FIkKKi14ElE
7. Jason Max Ferdinand Singers, *Holy City*, https://youtu.be/dzR3g-I_oRo
8. Jason Max Ferdinand Singers, *Didn't It Rain*, https://youtu.be/k2-vPED7Gho
9. Jason Max Ferdinand Singers, *O Praise the Lord*, https://youtu.be/iufJO4fwOs4
10. Jason Max Ferdinand Singers, *He's Got the Whole World in His Hands*, https://youtu.be/vdWTa7aB9iQ
11. Jason Max Ferdinand Singers, *Human Heart*, https://youtu.be/i7ydtWjiudU
12. Jason Max Ferdinand Singers, *Safe in His Arms*, https://youtu.be/ooAzImoc0cg

7 Choral Organizations
Resurrecting Song

Interviewees

Hilary Apfelstadt, former Interim Executive Director, American Choral Directors Association
Catherine Dehoney, President & CEO, Chorus America
Dominick DiOrio, Past President, National Collegiate Choral Organization
Kellori R. Dower, President, National Collegiate Choral Organization
Allen Henderson, Executive Director, National Association of Teachers of Singing
Robyn Hilger, Executive Director, American Choral Directors Association
Brian Lynch, Public Relations Manager, Barbershop Harmony Society
Jane Ramseyer Miller, Artistic Director, GALA (LGBTQ) Choruses
Tim Sharp, former Executive Director, American Choral Directors Association
Andre Thomas, Past President, American Choral Directors Association
James Weaver, Director of Performing Arts and Sports, the National Federation of State High School Associations

Introduction

The choral field is fortunate to have professional organizations that provide opportunities for professional development, support, and community. One of the significant stories of the pandemic was the Skagit Valley Chorale rehearsal that turned tragic. Consequently, choral singing was deemed a COVID-19 superspreader activity. Professional choral organizations immediately responded to calm the ensuing panic with information. A historic collaboration among these organizations during the COVID-19 pandemic resulted in the funding and commissioning of two vital aerosol studies. Their willingness to work together and speak with one voice saved lives and the choral art. This chapter reveals their behind-the-scenes dedication to resurrecting song.

DOI: 10.4324/9781003330486-8

What were your organization's plans when the COVID-19 pandemic emerged in March 2020?

James Weaver: I remember, we [National Federation of State High School Associations] were going as normal, and 2020 was a fascinating year for schools. It was a robust year. Our attendance rates for every event were up across the spectrum in every activity in every state. I was actually at the ASTA [American String Teachers Association] conference in Orlando in March of 2020, and I had gotten COVID-19 at that conference. By no means am I blaming ASTA, but it was one of those things where everyone's like, "Should we be in the room? Should we not be in the room?" It was right on the edge because that conference ended on March 11th. We couldn't even do proper testing because we're saving those tests for higher risk candidates. But they tested me for everything else, and they said, "Well, you're a clinical positive case. We can't waste a test on you because we're pretty sure you're not going to die from it." …

Also, we just kind of watched it in terror a little bit. From athletics to performing arts, we were watching groups that were playing in large-group contests in March. Suddenly, they delayed the morning, and the afternoon was canceled…. They couldn't finish the festivals. We had some All States [music festivals] that were halfway through that ended up getting pulled. The same thing was happening with basketball tournaments. All these things were happening so fast, and it was a scary thing to watch.

Tim Sharp: The [Skagit Valley Chorale] article had come out in the LA Times,[1] and we [American Choral Directors Association] had got this word about a superspreader. We were in Spokane [for the Northwest ACDA Conference], so we were in the same state where this happened. I was in the room with Brian Galante, Stan McGill, Amy Fuller, and that crew, and we were just sweating it. We were just like, "What are we doing?" I called the mayor. I called the county health organization. The city schools had not shut down. Nobody had thought about masks. I mean, masks weren't even in the vocabulary. I had not heard the words "social distancing" and then, on Friday, the governor said those words, "social distance." At that point, it was clear to me [that] the way those choirs were rehearsing, the way our honor choir kids were there, I just said, "We can't do it." ... I was looking for a sign, either a sign from God or a sign from the government or something and that was it.

We had choirs coming over the [mountain] pass. Gary Weidenaar's choir was on its way. We were on the phone to him trying to say, "Come or do you go back home?" We said, "Keep coming" on Thursday. Then by Friday, we were making phone calls and saying, "Stay home. Don't come to the conference because we're going to close it tonight." Then I called Vic Oakes [Southern ACDA Past President] in Mobile and said, "Vic, we're shutting down up here." He had started getting word from choirs that their superintendents and principals were saying, "We're not going to go [to the ACDA Conference]." He'd already had to substitute conductors for the masterwork that they were doing....

At that point, it just became a tsunami of realization, "We need to shut down." There was a lot of anger. At that point, it wasn't political. It was just confusion. We really, really sweated the decisions but I just couldn't make it more clear that we couldn't social distance and perform the way we were performing. So that was it.... We started on Wednesday. By Thursday, we shut it down. On Friday, Mobile had decided that they would shut it down Friday night. There was no Saturday performance. In Mobile, I stood up in front of the group and I said, "Folks, this may be the last live music you hear for a long time." ... That next morning, I caught my flight back to Oklahoma City.... Four days later, I got COVID-19, one of the first cases. I'm sure I got it in Mobile. I didn't talk about it because, at that time, it would have felt very, very condemning ... We got through all seven division conferences, so there was no negative at that point in terms of the finances or most of the performances.

Catherine Dehoney: Coincidentally, Liza Beth and Christie McKinney (from Chorus America) had been at an ACDA regional conference in Arkansas. All this stuff was coming out and choruses had canceled their travel. There was too much panic going on around them, and they were being affected. We had started thinking about it while they were sitting at their booth in ACDA. I never thought it was going to be short. I wasn't thinking, "In two weeks, we'll be back." What I remember doing is starting to research leading through change and crisis management. Really, what it all boiled down to was—the staff and I had a big meeting pretty much the day we shut down. So, people weren't coming in the office anymore. We were moving to remote work. Luckily, we were pretty well set up for that. We started thinking about focusing on our "true North."

Dominick DiOrio: What we [National Collegiate Choral Organization] decided to do immediately was respond to the moment and create a series of COVID-19-related webinars.[2] We had two sessions, all of which are still on the NCCO website. The first one was sort of immediate responses. I think there were four of them once a week like, "Aah, we're all at home. We need to do something and gather and just figure out what life is like." ... People needed, especially early on in 2020, to be around the people who were facing the same challenges as them. And so, for us, that was, "Singing is dangerous. What we do could kill people." We have to rely on technologies that very few of us are experts in. We suddenly have to become video engineers as well as audio engineers as well as conductors. We need to find a way to connect with our students that helps them to feel mentally well and balanced. We have to be able to, especially early on, not get burned out ourselves because doing all of the work is a huge burden.

Brian Lynch: We [Barbershop Harmony Society] were right in the middle of our annual cycle. Our annual cycle as an international organization organizes around our midwinter convention in January and our main international convention in July. In March, April,

	and May, we would have been hosting our preliminary rounds, qualification rounds, for quartets, for example. I think we squoze in two or three maybe before the pandemic.
Jane Ramseyer Miller:	GALA Choruses had a huge LGBTQ+ choral festival planned for 2020 in Minneapolis.[3] The organization depends on revenue from that quadrennial Festival and had already made deposits to all the venues, I mean, big venues: Orchestra Hall, Convention Center, local churches, and seven hotels. So, it was a big crisis within GALA to make the decision to postpone until 2021 and then to eventually cancel completely.
Allen Henderson:	2020 was a conference year, and we [NATS] were in planning mode for our summer national conference in Knoxville, Tennessee. In addition, spring is a very heavy time for NATS student auditions, which annually involve over 15,000 singers. We had been having behind-the-scenes conversations for several months prior to March mostly focused on contingency planning. In December, we were already talking and discussing many "What ifs?" because there were COVID-19 cases happening in other parts of the world. We had to discuss answers to questions like, "Can we go virtual? Are we going to cancel?" and address the many other components of live events.

In the midst of all of these conversations, of course, we were fielding all the questions from chapter presidents and regional governors about all of their planned events for the spring. We quickly worked with our web developers to add functionality and videos instead of coming to sing live auditions. We shifted and adjusted all our regulations and processes. And, of course, by March, we—myself, Tim Sharp, Catherine Dehoney from Chorus America, Marty Monson from Barbershop Harmony Society, and a couple of others—had been meeting basically weekly about all of the potential challenges before us. This became the core team that began collaborating on the many webinars[4] that we produced.

What challenges did your organization have to overcome? How did your focus and plans change to meet those challenges?

Henderson: We held our very first online chat[5] about what was happening in early March, with leaders of our organization and a variety of people that we invited. We advertised it and said, "All y'all come." It was a temperature check, "Let's chat, see how people are feeling, what's going on in our community."

After that event, I called Tim Sharp, and we had a long talk. The most important thing to me, and he agreed, was that we speak with one voice, have the necessary conversations across organizations within the singing space, and that we agree on parameters so that the messages that we, as singing organizations, are sending out in the world have cohesiveness and speak as much as possible with one voice about the data, what is coming, and how we want to advise people to handle all the issues that must be addressed. At this point, he and I then pulled in Marty from Barbershop Harmony Society and Catherine from Chorus America. Then, I contacted the president of the Performing Arts Medicine Association (PAMA) and NATS member, Dr. Lucinda Halstead. NATS already had a cooperative relationship with PAMA as well. We started meeting regularly and mapping out some ideas. We shared our thoughts and ideas with our communities in a coordinated manner. To me, this was the seminal decision that resulted in the success that we had during the pandemic in working with the singing community. We met early and agreed that we were going to be in regular conversation with one another ... and that we were going to rely on data, and bring in the best experts we could to advise us and our community.

Additionally, there was the University of Colorado study that ultimately ended up being managed by Mark Spede and James Weaver. We all agreed to support that initiative in addition to many, many, many other organizations. There was a separate study that also started at Colorado State University a bit later but deeper in aerosol data study. I was invited to serve on the scientific advisory committee for that study. They had a larger group of people that they ran through the protocols. It took longer but the results of that have been really very helpful because they also were a huge mask testing lab for the nation and for the state of Colorado. They had significant equipment and capacity. Both of those studies were moving along in parallel to our work, and those have proven to be very important, but we knew from the beginning that nothing was going to be immediate from those. They both moved a lot faster than normal scientific studies would but as with most research of this type, there was a time lag. In the meantime, we were using some of those experts to give us the latest more general data about aerosols and what the research they had been conducting was revealing.

Sharp: Now the best news of all that was that we had become so technically savvy in the national office that working from home was not a problem. Then we began to realize that we really don't need that kind of office space. Everyone started realizing that brick and mortar might be expendable ...

And then, when it was decided in August that it [conference] was going to become virtual, at that point, I realized I kind of had my own personal moment to say, "This is the time for me to let go." Because we had the things in place to put together a virtual conference, I knew it was going to be a different game. Actually, at that point, it was not quite the same task as a live conference would be. I felt a real peace that I had kind of gotten to that point and that I could turn it over to the machine, if you will....

And the whole time, I'm talking to NATS. I'm talking to Chorus America. I'm talking to Barbershop Harmony. I'm talking to the Medical Associations. We're doing webinars and seminars and all kinds of things about how to do this technology, what problems come with synchronous recording, and how to make virtual this and that. We're just slinging the how-to's and best practices out while we're also monitoring health updates.... Of course, the webinar[6] that really went viral brought on the scientific community to say, "Folks, we're dealing with something here that is significant." I think that was the warning shot that really put people into a wake-up. Again, stages of grief. A lot of people were angered. A lot of people were shocked. A lot of people were living, some would say, in denial.... My question in the webinar was, "What can we do?"

Andre Thomas:	We had to figure out how choral music would fit during this pandemic. Then immediately, we went to, "Okay, ACDA needs to respond." We went in and asked a group of people to write what became a pretty good little manual for teachers and church choir directors, helping them figure out how to make music during this pandemic. Of course, the country was not unified, as you well know. In New Haven, CT and at Yale University, there were rigorous protocols that were developed by the team of scientists working with the CDC, while in the South, they may have been singing in auditoriums, without [protocols] ... We couldn't come across anything that applied to everybody. Choir directors went with whatever they encountered in their environment and then did the best to try to help. That's what the organization is about. I was faced in 2021 with the national conference that had to be totally online, and I had to ask myself and others, how do we make that national conference work?" I was so proud of the membership of ACDA. The members used the opportunity as a time for helping and encouraging others...it was so positive. And from online we could be in everyone's personal environments—the composers were online... the conductors were online. We got to see the choirs in their own environments...Tim Westerhaus, Northwest Region President, was in a ski outfit in the mountains, saying, "Welcome to the great state of Washington!" At a time when it felt like the world was falling apart, ACDA was trying to bring it all back together...addressing all thrown at us, so the membership could continue to make music in a very real world.
Apfelstadt:	ACDA leadership had already realized they had to switch the conference to virtual. That had happened in early August. After Tim Sharp's retirement, the Executive Committee called me in late August 2020 and asked if I would become interim executive director. Right away this conference format was on everybody's mind. Everybody just settled down and figured it out. As for COVID-19, that was the fall that if people were doing anything, they were doing Zoom rehearsals. They were looking all the time to ACDA and Chorus America, the different professional groups, for help. There was a lot going on, as we tried to gather resources and make sure

that people had access to those. There seemed to be so much uncertainty and almost constant flux.

When Tim was at ACDA, there was a nice relationship amongst the leaders of all the professional organizations, and there was a kind of ongoing exchange. The others contacted me right away and said, "Let's get together," so we had a Zoom meeting with all of the other leaders. Of course, COVID-19 management was a big topic: "How can we address this? How can we be most helpful to people?" and so forth. You know, we were all trying to make the situation as truthful to people as possible and also to be encouraging. We felt the more information they had, the better, whether it was, "This is how we're doing to mitigate it," or, "This is what we're doing." For example, "We're still trying to have rehearsals, but this is how we're accommodating things." There were people in different regions with different levels of COVID-19 compared to other locations. There certainly was a while when I thought almost nobody was going to choir in person, but they were finding other ways to have choral experiences. Even sharing that information, I think, was helpful to a lot of people....

We also did a lot of checking in with state leadership and with the regions. The National Board met more times last year than it had previously. I felt it was really important that we be in contact, even on Zoom. We had a quarterly event for state presidents, which they had not done previously, and that's continuing now. People really seem to appreciate it. Then we did a whole lot of webinars. At that time, they were well-attended. Now I think people are done with that medium. I felt I needed to know who the people in ACDA were and what their concerns were, but I also just loved watching how they interacted with each other. We did some student events where the student chapters shared that they were doing amazing things. Their whole goal was to encourage each other because they weren't in regular classes in person, checking in with other people; they needed to find other ways to interact, and they did.

The 2021 national conference committee was astounding in the way they worked. One thing after another would change. I remember Stan McGill—he must have redone that schedule ten times. Everybody wanted it to work but we had no idea until the last minute about attendance, and whether the event would even pay for itself. There were big financial risks. It was scary because ACDA's budget model has been that the national conference would essentially pay for two years of operational funding. We had a huge bill from the hotels in Dallas when we had to cancel, regardless of force majeure. It was almost a million dollars in penalties from the hotels. Had we had to pay that, essentially, we could've gone bankrupt. Well, that wasn't going to happen! Then we started seeing people's registrations come in, and that was exciting, not only because we thought, "Oh, maybe [Laughs] it's going to pay for some of our costs; we'll recoup our expenses." Then just watching the comments people shared at concerts, something I normally would never do, was amazing. I wouldn't be at a concert talking to you online ... but you could see people's excitement in their comments about hearing groups, recognizing the sacrifices they had made to make those videos, just celebrating hearing and seeing people making music. People were thrilled to be talking about music. That was really, really exciting. I think everybody was very fulfilled by that. We ended up with 3,600 registrants, which was a really good outcome for a virtual conference.

Dehoney: What is true North for Chorus America? What does that mean for our organization and how do we keep going? What are we anticipating? The staff agreed that true North was about serving our members and supporting them. What are choruses going to need right now? The biggest thing that came up was information,[7] information, information, which was hard to get. It was changing all the time. That's when I started meeting with peers in the performing arts association world, such as the Performing Arts Alliance, but especially ACDA, Barbershop Harmony Society, NATS, and PAMA (Performing Arts Medical Association). We shared what we knew and where our organizations could get information about safety protocols, crisis planning, budgeting, and what to do about fundraising when things were so uncertain. Allen Henderson of NATS spearheaded the first webinar we did together. That happened at the beginning of May 2020—I call it the *infamous* webinar because of the ripple effects afterward! By that time, we were beginning to get a handle on what was really happening and at stake. Especially as the full story about the Skagit Valley Chorale was shared, we were beginning to see how everyone was responding and what this could mean for our field in terms of reputation, finances, audience's nervousness about singing and singers, and singers' nervousness about dealing with other singers. That was all very, very real.

The highs were high, and the lows were low! The good thing was the webinar gathered together experts who had information in one place. It was helpful that ACDA, Chorus America, Barbershop, and NATS were all trying to say the same thing and avoid adding to the confusion and misinformation going around. Each of the organizers was responsible for one piece of the webinar. My piece was data being collected on audience attitudes, disaster preparedness, and recovery. We were focused on presenting the latest information available.

One of the challenging segments was the part focusing on viral spread; nobody knew in advance exactly what the scientists were going to say on the webinar, and the recommendations ended up being very serious and rather a shock. For example, Dr. Lucinda Holstead [of Medical University of South Carolina] said, in essence, "Choruses, you're not going to be able to sing safely, unless you do these major safety mitigations." At that stage of the pandemic, those things she identified to prevent viral spread were nearly impossible for a chorus to do.

Afterward, chorus leaders reacted one of two ways. Either they were furious with comments like, "By sharing this information so publicly, you (Chorus America, ACDA, etc.) are destroying the choral field," or they said, "Thank you so much. We appreciate this and apply this to our own situation and the needs of our own choral families." They immediately focused on what they could do safely to keep singing. Those who were, understandably, angry and scared took longer to get to, "Now what *can* we do?" but eventually they did get there. According to our research, very few choruses stopped activity altogether. And, best of all, I haven't heard of many choruses going out of existence completely due to the pandemic. Most modified their activities, such as singing outside. Chorus leaders have told me, "We did less. We didn't get together as often. We did Zoom socials, but we sang spread out in a garage." The larger the chorus' budget size, the more likely they were to do virtual performances or string together past performances and present them as virtual content. I was very impressed that so many children and youth choruses moved quickly online and didn't stop serving their young singers for very long.

The other way Chorus America was able to help was to share information with the choral field about the emergency funding that was available. Previously, the majority of choruses were unlikely to have applied for federal funding in their history. They tend to think of themselves as too small and too grassroots. This time, I think 70% of those that answered our chorus operations survey had applied and received federal emergency funding. I think in the long run that's going to be a good thing. Perhaps they will find future opportunities for federal funding.

Miller: GALA Choruses wasn't eligible for PPP or grant assistance.... 7,000 people were registered to attend the festival and GALA put out a request to any delegates that could donate their registration fees back. It was huge, something like 60% of delegates donated their registrations. Choruses also donated their chorus registration, and it kept the organization alive. Without that, GALA would have folded or at least gone on hiatus for a long time. Eventually, the decision was that Festival 2021 also seemed too iffy. It was too risky to go forward and have to cancel again so the next Festival will be in 2024. That was when we set a goal of trying to do virtual events during that festival year. We started monthly in January 2021 with 45–60 minute events. During the original festival week, we had a virtual event every day.

GALA Choruses may be unique from other choruses. Queer choruses are very much a family for people, their church, their synagogue, their communities of faith. When that falls away and you can't see those people in person, it's a big crisis. People already in the queer community struggle with anxiety, depression, and all kinds of mental health issues, and we wanted to provide ways for people to connect in whatever ways we could.

Lynch: I guess the pandemic hit the second or third week of March, and we held on to some hope of holding our national conference up into early May. We went ahead and canceled. We'd been scheduled for Los Angeles in 2020, and that was going to be a big deal. That was going to be our first international competition that had performers on stage who were not men.... We ended up that summer, I guess we'll say Innovation #1, having an online international convention. It was in a virtual space called Virbela, so it was like walking around inside a video game. It was not a terribly satisfying singing experience for anybody, but our organization is half a singing organization and half a community—just a loving community of people who want to see each other and be next to each other. By that measure, you still were bumping into people, in the nature of a virtual world. It wasn't all that organized. You wandered around like, "James! How are you, man?" ...

Our summertime major education event, Harmony University, normally 700 people coming to a week-long school in Nashville at Belmont University, was shifted all online.... We programmed in our keynote speeches and programmed in nightly fun activities, little breakout things, teach-a-tag, teach casual singing. As you know, it's hard to enjoy singing all by yourself facing your Zoom screen, but it was better than not singing.

We had another event in the summer of 2020. We did a virtual online battle of the classics quartet contest. We called it the *Legacy Quartet Contest*,[8] and it was all the quartets that had never won the international championship, all the second-place quartets. We had the content streaming on YouTube Live for free but then we also had a premium product where you could pay for access to a Zoom chat to watch along with your heroes....

In the fall of 2020, we started a two-hour fast-paced variety hour called *Barbershop Live @ Home*, a virtual national chapter meeting on Zoom. We had speakers. We had teach-a-tag, learn something together led by a rock-star, had a history presentation by our historian, and did a performance breakdown—like watching a video together and breaking down the performance. We ended up doing a series of four of those monthly, and our attendance just grew. For a two-hour Sunday night free show, we were hitting about 450–475 attending live and interacting.... After the formal programming was done, we said, "Okay, everyone. Grab a beer. It's sit back and chitchat time."

DiOrio: We had some others [webinars] that happened. At that point, we weren't sure what the conference would be. We weren't sure when the pandemic would end but we knew we didn't have any commitments for our 2021 conference. So, unlike other organizations where they had hotel contracts, we weren't liable for anything like that. We had the chance to sort of step back and say, "Okay, since we're in sort of a financially safe place, how can we think about how best to serve our membership?"

We also took a step back and met with our national board for the first time ever virtually. The way NCCO works is, we have an executive board of five or six individuals, and then we have a national board of 50. The national board is the sort of governing authority, the legislative body of the organization, but typically, they had only ever met at the conference the night before the sessions began. So, we were like, "Well, this is silly. We now are all used to video conferencing." We met our national board for the first time in May of 2021 to sort of get their feelings and feedback. And then, we started, after June of 2020, a strategic planning process to help build a more anti-racist organization in particular.

We brought Reverend Doctor Jamie Washington in to work with our board in August of 2020 where we had a full-day summit of training for all of our national and executive board members. We followed that up with a panel of BIPOC individuals, predominantly African American, that Elizabeth Swanson moderated as part of our next series of webinars. That led to our membership survey in the fall of 2020, which led directly to the creation of our vision and mission governance committee, which became the sort of thought leader committee that helped to set forth a new mission, actually our first mission and vision for the organization. We had a purpose before with our founding members in 2004 but that was sort of paramount to us. We knew that we had grown up as an organization and it was time for us to really think about who we wanted to be going forward. And because we had so much data, the member survey report was published on the website,[9] the results of our two task forces that helped to talk about the conference and the mission. I tried to be as transparent as possible about sharing the information we've gathered and about our thought process that the board was able to, in May of 2021, approve the new mission and vision, which was great. It set us on a path to then move into where we are now....

We had been doing that work [DEIA] gradually, but we had never articulated to our membership that we were doing it. And so, what did that mean? That meant that, one, they didn't know unless we told them, first of all. So, they would have no way of knowing we're doing this work. And two, it was not a part of our sort of governing philosophy. It just happened to be the values of the people who were elected, which meant that it wasn't systemic. If we wanted these things to continue, if these were really important to us, then we had to make sure they were a guiding part of our philosophy and our values, which is what led, ultimately, to the strategic planning process, which we were going to begin doing anyway. But once we were all in lockdown, we suddenly had no other things on our plate that were as vital as that....

At that point, they also said, in May of 2021, "Yes, an in-person conference is what we want." And so, we started planning in May of 2021 for an in-person conference at Morehouse College, which would have been the first conference at an HBCU (Historically Black Colleges and Universities). We were thrilled. We went down to visit. At that point, May of 2021, the mask mandates were ending, and life was looking great. Delta wasn't really a thing and Omicron didn't exist yet. We were truly thinking that "Okay, this is going to be our great regathering." ... We first postponed it to January, but we still opened registration because that's what seemed like the right thing to do. And then, of course, the height of the Omicron wave was in the middle of January, and that became clear to us on December 30th ... David Morrow (Morehouse College Glee Club and the Academic Program Director for Music and Theater and Performance) called me. He was like, "Morehouse is going to announce today that there can't be anyone on campus until the end of January." We were like, "Okay, so, now the decision has been made for us, which is good."

Hilger: Within the first month [of being executive director], I asked Andre [Thomas] to call the national board together. I said, "We have got to put a foundation in place for COVID-19 guidance for the conferences from day one because we cannot have this volatility every single day everywhere you are in the country. People need to know what they're agreeing to when they agree [to come to an in-person conference]. We need to avoid all of the financial implications of having people's money. Then you got to refund them, which every time you're doing that, you're incurring credit card charges, staff time charges" ...

We sort of knew more about what we were doing by the time we got to October 2021. It was just ensuring that we did it. I put together a proposal for the national board and said, "Here's my recommendation about how we triage this from the get-go. We put mandated masking in place for all people regardless of where you are in the country. The end." That is the foundation because we know the lay of the land is different all across the country.... Then on top of that, region presidents had the ability to build any other guidance that they wanted. And then in the last layer, you had to enforce whatever the state, county, city, and venue mandates were.... So, I spent my first six months at ACDA being the *COVID-19 Queen*.

In every region, with the exception of Southern, attendance was down. However, it was not so far down that it was like, "We should not have had an in-person conference." ... Every region had the financial resources to weather the storm. What I kept telling the region presidents was, "Even if it costs us money this year to run conferences, it will be an investment in propelling the profession forward...".

While we may be sort of in a new normal, we're way more equipped to know how to live here now. There really isn't a point in arguing with people anymore about what they're going to do related to their vaccination or masking or any of those things. We have to maintain the expectation and we have to move forward. People will opt in or out based on whatever they're doing. We can do that in a kind and non-judgmental way from a transparency standpoint....

By the time we got to the Western and Northwestern [conferences], we said, "We will continue to monitor the community spread in each of these locations. We will make the decision based on what is happening but again, this is the floor." ... And in fact, on the last day of the Western Conference, Long Beach did not have a mask [mandate]. The city released its mandate, and they were in low transmission. It was not that way on Friday morning. By Friday mid-afternoon, they had changed it, and we actually allowed the choirs on Friday evening to sing without a mask. That is how fast the guidance was changing....

I'm not going to tell you that it wasn't rough because it was. Operationally in the regions, there were in different places choirs that were supposed to perform whose universities or schools would not allow them to travel. So, programs changed, like, Texas schools coming to Southwestern [conference]. The State of Texas said, "You cannot mandate masks within any level of schools or any of those things." ... So, maybe that was the most challenging piece, as it was not like one thing was happening in one place. When people would call and contact us, we had to be really careful about saying, "Where are you? What region are you going to?" all along to make sure that we could support them in the right way....

There's a larger implication for ACDA, though, that we are going to actually not recognize even until 2025. When we pivoted to the virtual conference in 2021, we were under contract in the city of Dallas (hotels, venues, all of those things) completely under contract into 2021. The cost to get out of those contracts was almost a million dollars, $990,000. Through really great work, they ... (and this was before my time), renegotiated those contracts into 2025. So, we are going to Dallas in 2025. It'll be public but how that happened was moving from 2021 on a decision that actually was made way back in 2016. Here's the real challenge. When we were under contract and going to Dallas, at that time they had not leveraged their no gender-neutral restrooms. They had not leveraged their lack of gender care that they've recently done. They had not had open carry from a gun perspective. They did not have the abortion restrictions that they have in place now. All of those things are going to rub up against our ADEI values and it's still going to cost us a million dollars to do anything differently and we don't have it. ACDA will go bankrupt.... So, I'm not going to say like when we get to 2025 that it's going to be over, but it is likely to be sort of such a blip on the radar that when we get to 2025 and people are irritated about being in Dallas that there will be no perspective ... That decision was made in 2016.... So, we will still have

COVID-19 impact on ACDA in 2025, but it won't look like COVID-19 impact. When we get to 2025 and ask, "Why is attendance down?" People will likely say, "It's all these political things in Texas," which is likely to be true, but how we got there was actually directly related to being in the middle of COVID-19 in 2021.

Weaver: Because the schools were shut down, my world really shifted to revolve around copyright compliance. So, I asked myself, "What are you going to do for the rest of the year? Everyone's virtual learning. How are we going to be copyright compliant in all this?" I got to work with publishers and record labels and all these different organizations, all while battling COVID-19, which is not the smartest way to do this.... In March [2020], we had drafted guidance about instrument cleanliness for when everybody was going back because, remember, the first shutdown of schools was supposed to be for two weeks, and so we had geared up guidance to help from what we knew at the time. At the time we didn't know anything, and the CDC (Centers for Disease Control and Prevention) didn't know anything. Everybody's talking about contact surfaces for transmission, so we worked with a bunch of manufacturers. The NFHS and NAMM (National Association of Music Merchants) and NAFME (National Association for Music Education), joined together and put out the instrument cleaning guidelines. [It] Turns out that wasn't the problem....

On the copyright work, I had contacted 400 plus publishers and had received permissions[10] from all of them to allow us to do virtual stuff, such as music sharing for the rest of the 2020 year, and also for the 2020–2021 school year. We still have 410 plus publishers that gave all of us permission, so that's a huge shout-out to those guys, because without those permissions we really would have been stuck with what to do in virtual learning.

Then in April the famous webinar happened, where everybody's like, "Oh, no music in school for two years!" That's where I turned off the webinar and said, "This is unacceptable. There's got to be a way we can solve this problem." So, the next day, Dr. Mark Spede [Director of Bands and Professor, Clemson University] called me, and he's like, "Hey, I just got done reading 300 articles on respiratory disease transmission. Here's the folder. Read them. Let's see what we're going to do." My reaction was, "Uh, all right." I sat down and, in 36 hours, read all these articles. I was like, "Yeah, I think this thing is definitely airborne. It's definitely an aerosolized transmission." So, Mark and I sat down and started with, "Let's assume it's airborne and the world hasn't caught up to it yet." This was three months before scientists wrote the letter to the WHO (World Health Organization) asking them to officially make it an aerosol-based disease transmission. It all happened because Mark went down this rabbit hole of respiratory disease research, shared it with me, and I was like, "Let's create an action plan and let's tackle this thing."

By the time we got to the middle of April 2020, we had identified what we thought was the issue with particle size. We didn't know what the particle size was because we're not those people. Then Mark had a contact with an aerosol scientist through a contact in CBDNA (College Band Directors National Association). They recommended Dr. Shelly Miller, saying, "If you want someone to study this, she is the one to do it." So, we contacted Dr. Miller, which worked great as she is also an active musician of her own. She said, "Yes, I think you guys are spot-on. I think this is what we need to do. What do you need to see?" Mark and I explain what we think needs to happen. She said, "We can do that. The lab is currently closed but I think because of this research we can get them back open." This is April 2020. It was so fast and so crazy. Then we get through April. We're doing the design. She gives us a quote for the cost, "It's going to be $35,000." We said, "Okay, that's fine." The NFHS foundation kicked in $25,000. CBDNA kicked in $10,000. We're like, "Let's do it today." She's like, "All right. I need all of your design specifications and what you want people to play, sing, how many times we want to test it," and all that kind of stuff. "Sweet," we sat down over the weekend and put all that together. She's like, "This is going to be $100,000." Mark and I replied, "Okay, let's do that. We'll get $100,000." Then the weekend passes. I called Mark and I'm like, "We're going to have replicate this thing. We can't just do one lab." Mark replied, "Ah, okay." So, we called Shelly back and said, "All right, Dr. Miller. Here we go. We need to replicate." She said, "Great, I know the person to do it. It's going to be Dr. Jelena Srebric over at University of Maryland in College Park." We're like, "Okay." Shelly, Mark, and I get on a call. We call Jelena. She replied to our idea, "Yes, I think you guys are on the right track. We don't have the same equipment that Boulder has, which is good, so we're going to test it from two different directions and see if we get the same result." We thought, "This is perfect." Then Dr. Srebric said, "It's $125,000 on my end to do this design experiment." Shelly agreed, "Yeah, it's probably closer to $125,000 on our end, too, because we're going to have to hire some more staff to do this." Now we're up to a quarter million dollars and Mark and I have $35,000 secured. Then we keep going through, "All right, we also need to do this and this. And have we thought about this?" By the time we're all done, the price tag is closer to $330,000, and we are 10% of the way there. This is the end of April. So now we start in May and decide it's time to activate everybody in the performing arts. We called everybody that we knew, and then we called everybody that they knew. In 21 days, we had created a coalition of 125 organizations that fully funded the entire study, with a huge shout-out to NAMM. On May 2nd of 2020, NAMM came and said, "We will match the funds up to $140,000." So, we're like, "Okay, done." That gave us a huge boost to really go after it. Our music merchants really are what made the aerosol study happen because they supplied the funding for us to get the rest of it. But in 21 days, by May 21st, we had all of the money we needed…. We've never had this kind of coalition before. It was incredibly rewarding.

We let the labs do their work in May and June. Mark and I put a lot of pressure on the science teams because they said this kind of work would typically take a year to 18 months to do. We're like, "Great, we have about a month to a month and a half to get it done because if we don't have results out before August 1st, we're not going to have music coming back into the schools." So going back to that famous webinar, they're like, "We're two years out." And we're like, "We're going to do it in six months. From March to September, we want music back in schools." What's hanging up the return to music was the Skagit Valley Chorale incident that happened in

Washington. So many people were saying, "Music is the worst thing in this pandemic," which technically isn't true. It is one of the higher aerosolization activities we have, but by far it's not even the worst thing you can do in a pandemic like this....

What we did was, we gave them weeks. So, they went to the lab. Tehya Stockman, one of the graduate assistants (she's getting her doctoral degree in aerosol sciences), was probably in the lab 12–14 hours a day every day, just cranking through experiments, crunching data, and getting data to people to review ... So, for every instrument, every voice, they did the mitigations for the masking. Then, for the distancing, at that time, the CDC was saying six feet, but we knew it was more likely three feet because we were stopping so much of it from coming out. The stuff that did come out was definitely hitting the ground within three feet. Then with the increased ventilation and reduced amount of time, we were not getting this buildup of anything. So, by July 13th of 2020, we had the first of our recommendations out.[11] We refined those again in August. In November of 2020 we had our final list of recommendations, which if we have an issue today, we go right back to the November 2020 ones and say, "This is exactly what you do." Basically, within that six-month period of time from shutdown to conceptualization, we went from having no people in in-person music to having four and a half million students back in secondary music education. Then we ended the 2021 school year.

Then we came out in mid-August with a refinement, really a "Okay, here's exactly how you make this stuff. Here's exactly how you create the mitigations to reduce risk. Here is how you calculate your room airflows." Then in November, because the science study teams kept going, they were testing and retesting from the preliminary information in July and August, we had refined the science and were basically ready to publish information by November. So, when we had November information come through, that was like, "Okay, we know exactly [what it] looks like," because we'd gotten Schlieren tests that show how the air moves in a room. We have laser sheet imagery. We finally had CFD (computational fluid dynamics) modeling that was able to track every air molecule in the room. It'd taken two weeks for a supercomputer to process the CFD data. So, we knew a ton by November but some of it took more time and we had to get the school year going. But we were happy that their initial results were good, and then we just needed to refine them from there....

But when it turned political, that's really when our job actually became more difficult, because we had teachers who were like, "For my own safety, I want to require this, but now in my state or in my school I'm no longer able to require these things, so what do I do?" That became more difficult for us to navigate because, like I mentioned before, we can stop the virus at the source, but once it's out, it's much harder to stop. An N95 mask is really good at keeping those things inside, but it's not as good at keeping them out. Those blue surgical masks, they're good at keeping your particles in at 80%, but to stop particles coming into the mask, it's only 50%. That's really where it became a big switch in the policy and kind of away from science and toward the political, and that was more difficult.

How did you keep hope alive for your members? What did you do to help them cope with not being able to sing?

Apfelstadt: We started publishing every Wednesday some silver lining commentaries in emails to the membership. I would ask people to contribute. We lined them up over about 15 weeks where they would write about something they had done, or how they experienced an unexpected positive outcome. Sundra [Flansburg] was great about helping us get that material out because part of her job in membership was to make sure that people had weekly emails that told them, among other things, what resources they could find on the website.[12] For example, we shared the information that was coming from the Colorado research study, and from the CDC, because we felt it was important and ACDA was supporting it. It was a combination of saying, "Here's the research. These are the things that have been written and these are people's life experiences." That was very important. There were lots of conversations going back and forth. In some of the Facebook groups (like "I'm a Choir Director"), there was lots of ACDA input. Sometimes there were situations—and this is going to happen because it's social media—where someone would post something that was just off-the-charts wrong. I would have staff looking for those instances, and I notice Robyn Hilger still does that. It was especially important that ACDA's information was fact-based and accurate during the pandemic.

Dower: We hope that what we've presented and what we provided in our programming with the webinars have been helpful, but the jury's kind of still out on whether or not people found it helpful. We have some scarce data that folks did enjoy and appreciated through … We are continuing to try to find out different ways to get the message out and to help support collegiate choirs and their conductors. To that extent, I think we've been as successful as we could be in this environment.

Lynch: We were offering resource guides and a little bit on meeting planning. In the very, very first weeks, we started some programming emanating from Harmony Hall, so we had *Free Fridays* where we just loaded up. We did a four-hour block on Friday afternoon of five, six, and seven classes that were casual drop-in kind of things, just to provide some kind of barbershop fix. Those were well-subscribed. It was also free to our members. More than anything we needed to throw a lifeline to say, "Barbershop's going to stay alive."

Is there anything your organization did or learned during the pandemic that it would like to keep post-pandemic?

Dower: A goal of mine is to bring more collegiate choral conductors in so that we can support and help them. I also want to see more support for students that are in collegiate choirs. We don't know who the next collegiate choral conductor is, so I want to make sure that we provide some support. To that end, instead of a graduate choral conducting program that we normally hold in person (we did have some that we selected to work with Dr. Anton Armstrong), we matched up conductors with a national board member as a mentor. We meet with them for a half-an-hour session to go over some things that they think are important and to give them feedback. Even though they weren't selected, we still want to provide some support to them. One of the final things that we're doing as an initiative beyond our membership drive is we are reimagining messaging and marketing.

Lynch: I believe deeply that we'll never ever be afraid of Zoom again. I think that's going to continue for a lot of people for a long, long time. Going the other direction, when some groups were starting to meet in person, masked, distanced and in safe settings, but their distant coaches couldn't travel to them, we got accustomed to, "Yep, there's our coach on the big screen on Zoom." Everyone's gotten over the tech hurdle now. We found out, we could do it, and do it well, and it could possibly be satisfying. Those old guys that everyone said were never going to pick up on the tech? They totally owned the tech after just a few weeks.

Henderson: I think the pandemic has permanently changed the way we will do some things in our profession. It has affirmed that we CAN do what we do in ways we didn't think we could before. Certainly, in the voice teaching community the predominant pre-pandemic response to teaching online would be, "I could never teach a voice lesson on Zoom or remotely. My student must be in front of me." Even the most technophobic person, when driven by the need to make a living and do what they love, came forward and said, "Oh, yeah. I have to figure it out. I'm not very good at this, but we're going to get it." Those who teach voice to professional singers or are traveling all the time are checking in from the road now more than they ever did before and even having regular lessons remotely. The work on low latency performance technologies and singing technologies was really transformational and will continue to be so in the future. That's going to continue to impact the global industry of singing for a long time to come, and it's also going to provide some interesting creative outlets for people.

Sharp: I think our pedagogy may have taken an improvement in some areas because we really had to break things down into increments that could be delivered through this kind of medium, which wasn't bad. We couldn't make assumptions about steps. We had to put lesson plans into sequential things. We had to be able to measure it in ways that we didn't measure before. That's nothing but good. I also think we learned the value of community. If we never knew how important what we do as a choir is, in terms of community, we know now that community is hugely important in the lives of people because we lost it.

Apfelstadt: I've heard this from enough people, and I've seen it myself, to think that one of the biggest things that we can do is to really focus on community-building. As a university professor,

I always had retreats and social gatherings with choirs. I felt it was important, but I think I would probably let them know even more now that there's a system in place that can be helpful to them apart from music. We know singers are needy coming out of the pandemic. I think we must look at people's entire picture of health. It's not just their musical health that matters. When I went to school, I think that's all the conductor cared about: "How's your voice? Can you sing the right notes today?" We've come so far beyond that; caring for the person as well as their musicianship is important. Another lesson relates to over-programming. Do we really need to do these long performances? Are we getting as much out of the music as we could or trying to cover too much? During the pandemic, especially with online concerts, we did less repertoire and that was all right. Coupled with that is the influence of George Floyd's murder and the importance of ADEIB that has kind of superimposed with COVID-19. In talking with people, I realize there's a powerful set of outcomes. My own programming for honor choirs has changed. We have shifted in our thinking about music and its role, I believe, or maybe we are just refocusing priorities.

Dehoney: I really do think so. I think the pandemic has changed how choruses and Chorus America talk about the field and how we advocate for ourselves. In addition to focusing on earned revenue, we have even more lived experience with how important choral singing is to a community, including all the benefits of choral singing that show up in other aspects of life: In health, emotional well-being, civic engagement, and social capital for communities. I think with the pandemic taking it all away or in most cases, it was the *threat* of taking it all away, people truly realized what they had. Most choruses really fought for it. The fact is nobody prefers to produce virtual choirs. For choral conductors, this was hell, but they did it for a while to help the chorus continue. I also think the fact that choruses had to be virtual for the most part helped open a wider audience that was looking for comfort and inspiration while staying at home. In the first year and a half, almost two years, many more people were open to watching and sharing virtual choral performances. I think it gave choruses the courage to think beyond their concert halls and open up this new area of work. It's not going to replace live performance. Being together, singing together, and doing live performances I believe will still be that engine of creativity, innovation, and spirit. What they can do virtually now becomes another area of work to reach new audiences and those previous audience members who may never come back to in-person concerts.

I also think there's something to be said for some of the health and safety protocols that were put in place that may come back in the middle of flu season. We lose singers all the time to flu and colds in the winter. Maybe for short periods of time, they'll ask everybody to mask up—such as in February in Washington, D.C.!

Hilger: Yes, for sure. I think the conference committees, national conference committee, and national board used to meet only physically on site about once a year. It cost mega money, six digits worth of money to move all of those people. There'll be 150 people here and you have to hotel them and travel them. Moving to the virtual format allows us to have much more access to people more often. The national board and the EC and meetings with the states and talking with the R&Rs (Repertoire and Resources) and all of this stuff through COVID-19 and now coming out of COVID-19 will be amplified. It will happen more often because everybody's attuned to the virtual format now, and this is a really great platform to convene people more regularly, which organizationally will really help us.... So, now, they are on a much more rigorous schedule and things are happening faster. You can see it.... I think that there's been a level of bonding among people who have done work during this time and that they will always be bonded together, and this will be really great for our organization. Because when people endeavor so deeply together, we will be able to harness that energy over and over and over again.... There's a level of generosity and hope and then also this sort of perseverance of making it through the pandemic....

I mean, you guys were facing literally the end of the profession as we knew it and people did not pull back from that conversation, which tells me that we can endeavor greatly during the toughest moments and figure it out. In that kind of pandemic learning, the thing that happened is you had to learn and grow across basically every sector.... And it wasn't just about conceptually understanding what was happening; there was an entirely new hard skill set that had to be learned, technical skills, planning skills, and so this learning curve is straight up.

Thomas: All the wonderful, supportive atmosphere we had during our national conference. I got to see so much of everybody else's stuff online, and it also allowed me to be encouraging and reinforcing for those people who were working all the time through

	the pandemic. It was difficult because it meant we were trying to do all these rehearsals online now. People with little financial support for technology were even more challenged.
Weaver:	One thing that came out of the pandemic, which was good, we started a state administrator meeting in early April of 2020. Every ten days we had an administrative staff meeting for all the state administrators that would log on, like, "What's happening in your state? How is this going?" We connected the states in ways that they'd never been connected before. And then now, "post-pandemic," we have those monthly meetings, and the states feel very connected. We're seeing a lot more best practices coming to fruition across all states.
	Another thing that happened was that there became more communication between teachers and administrators than what they've had before. I think that's something else we need to be able to keep … The more we can have that discussion between administrators and teachers, the more we can say, "Hey, you know what? Kids come to school to be in a music program or in a theater program or whatever." They don't obviously come to school for English class. Now, they stay in school for English class because we bring them to the building. That conversation, which has really started during the pandemic, it's always been there, but it got really hyped up in the pandemic because we're trying to get these classes back. I think those conversations should really remain, and have, by and large. That's no shade on English teachers, by the way.

Unprompted, some leaders reflected on the silver linings of the COVID-19 pandemic:

Apfelstadt:	Do you know that the highest percentage of membership that goes to national [ACDA] conferences is 27%? That's a statistic gleaned over time. In 2021, when we were online for the virtual conference, we had people who'd never been to any kind of national conference who signed up and were then able to see and hear some of these groups they hadn't experienced before; they could partake of such a wide array of things. That was a silver lining right there…. In this way, I think we reached people whom we wouldn't have reached otherwise. I was really proud of the staff, officers, and volunteers on that committee, how hard they worked to make that a successful musical experience. And the performers and presenters outdid themselves.

Thomas: You can never go to everything at an ACDA conference. You can't do it, but with it being virtual, they can see everything, when they want it, and how they want it. They didn't spend any money. [Laughs] We managed to keep that low. And lo and behold, we were in transition with having to go hire a new executive director, and we were worried about all the money. We thought we would have to go into Chapter 11 because we had to cancel the Dallas conference. So, we had just tons of concerns. So, it was a breath of fresh air.

The most extensive silver lining for me personally with my choirs was that I got to know the individual voices better than ever before. Every two weeks, they submit their video and audio recordings.

Lynch: When I said we added 18 choruses, I was being language-precise there, because a chorus is a singing ensemble inside a chapter, which is a governance unit. Most of those choruses that were added in the pandemic were women's and mixed. The ball was rolling on founding new ensembles, and then the pandemic came along, but that ball kept rolling. People kept founding their new mixed organizations within existing chapters. We did have two new brand-new sites, though, starting in the course of the pandemic. They came together and said, "We want to be a part of this organization. We'll get going, pandemic be damned."

Dehoney: The good news for choruses is their overhead is typically low because very few choruses own their own buildings and performance spaces. They are able to be pretty resilient. Since few concerts break even with ticket revenue, not being able to perform actually saved groups a lot of money.... Today, choruses continue to work on coming back to pre-pandemic norms; ticket sales, except for popular holiday concerts, are still down.

As for Chorus America itself, we received both rounds of emergency NEA (National Endowment for the Arts) funding and a PPP loan/grant. This, along with some special gifts from donors, kept us going and made it possible to offer pay-what-you-can membership dues during the past few years. We are doing OK, but like everyone else concerned about the coming years without emergency funding.

Miller: We often talk about the gifts of COVID-19 because there *were* gifts amidst the pain and the isolation. GALA Choruses had been working for six years with GALA's New Harmony Committee addressing equity, access, and belonging, and just before COVID-19 had created a workbook for choruses.[13] It's a self-guided workbook to help choirs engage in these conversations. All of a sudden, choirs couldn't rehearse, and many choirs picked up *A New Harmony Workbook*. And then, George Floyd was murdered, and choirs were longing for more conversation and tools. So, we saw dozens of choruses jump into those conversations which can actually work over Zoom.

Weaver: If you want to talk about one of the best things that happened, for me anyway, through the pandemic, was the coalition of aerosol study groups—125 organizations that have never really communicated before. There's communication and collaboration happening in that arena that's never been there before. It's exciting to see, and I hope we don't lose that because I really think that is a #1 thing that's going to continue to make music pretty strong as we go.

We also need to recognize that music was never super weak to begin with. When 98.5% of all schools have a music program, that's not a weak program. So, one of the things I think happened as well in the pandemic is our messaging started to shift a little bit, where we stopped saying, "Please don't cut. Please don't do this," to, "Hey, we have a strong program. You need to give us the tools to continue that program." I think that's much better messaging, and I think we're starting to see that change over the course of the pandemic as well. One of them is, I've stopped hearing my least favorite phrase, which is, "Music is more important now than ever." I went after it in a webinar that I think went viral a little bit. I was like, "Music is pretty damn important today. It should have been pretty damn important yesterday, and if we do things right, it's going to be pretty damn important tomorrow. So, let's take it for that." Then the other one was just thanking the music teachers for everything they did. Even though we went to work and got to town on all the stuff that happened in the aerosol study, the teachers are the ones who implemented it and fought for it and got their kids back in classrooms. We at any level cannot thank teachers who are in the classrooms enough for doing everything that they've done. I joked before the pandemic that if you want something done, you give it to a music teacher, and it'll get done. The pandemic proved that if you need something colossal done, you give it to a music teacher and it's going to happen. I just want to thank all music teachers for doing what they did over those two years.

Notes

1. Los Angeles Times, *A choir decided to go ahead with rehearsal. Now dozens of members have COVID-19 and two are dead*, https://www.latimes.com/world-nation/story/2020-03-29/coronavirus-choir-outbreak
2. NCCO, *NCCO Webinars*, https://ncco-usa.org/publications/ncco-webinars
3. GALA Choruses, *GALA Festival History*, https://galachoruses.org/galadev/events/gala-festival/festival-history/
4. NATS, *COVID-19 Resources*, https://www.nats.org/covid_resources.html#webinars
5. NATS, *Emergency NATS Chat: Calming the Coronavirus Crisis and Taking Your Teaching Online*, https://youtu.be/Uw8U5ULL40o
6. NATS, *A Conversation: What Do Science and Data Say About the Near Term Future of Singing*, https://youtu.be/DFl3GsVzj6Q
7. Chorus America, *Choruses and COVID-19 (Coronavirus)*, https://chorusamerica.org/resource/top-resource/choruses-covid-19-coronavirus
8. Barbershop Harmony Society, *The Legacy Quartet Championship*, https://www.barbershop.org/the-best-who-never-won-the-legacy-quartet-championship
9. NCCO, *Member Survey Report*, https://ncco-usa.org/publications/ncco-member-survey-report
10. NFHS, *Copyright Resources*, https://www.nfhs.org/articles/nfhs-copyright-resources/
11. NFHS, *Unprecedented International Coalition Led by Performing Arts Organizations to Commission COVID-19 Study*, https://www.nfhs.org/articles/unprecedented-international-coalition-led-by-performing-arts-organizations-to-commission-covid-19-study/
12. ACDA, *Pandemic-focused Resources*, https://acda.org/resources-for-choral-professionals-during-a-pandemic
13. GALA Choruses, *A New Harmony: Equity, Access, Belonging*, https://galachoruses.org/resource/a-new-harmony-equity-access-and-belonging/

Conclusion
We Sing On

In times of suffering, humanity has often turned to song to process communal trauma and create a path forward.[1] However, COVID-19 twisted singing, an instrument of healing, into a vector of disease. This project aimed to document the choral community's journey through this challenging time of change and aid it in rebuilding in a new era where COVID-19 is endemic. Specifically, this book focused on the following questions:

- How did the choral community respond to the challenges of the COVID-19 pandemic?
- What did the choral community do or learn from its time during the COVID-19 pandemic that it would like to retain post-pandemic?

Two themes emerged regarding the choral community's response to the COVID-19 pandemic: Collaboration and community. COVID-19 socially distanced the singers, but the solution to the survival of the choral arts was to collaborating in new ways. The choral community gathered online in Facebook groups to co-create learning plans and share virtual choir advice. When administrators sought to cut funding, new organizations, such as Chor Amor and Professional Choral Collective, were formed to produce new resources. In addition, guest teachers, vocal coaches, conductors, and composers virtually visited classrooms and rehearsals at an increased frequency to share expertise when the world went remote. However, more importantly, when it seemed that choral singing would cease for 24 months, professional choral organizations joined forces with the scientific community to commission COVID-19 aerosol research that allowed a safe return to singing within several months. "If you want to talk about one of the best things that happened, for me anyway, through the pandemic, was the coalition of aerosol study groups—125 organizations that have never really communicated before. There's communication and collaboration happening in that arena that's

DOI: 10.4324/9781003330486-9

never been there before. It's exciting to see, and I hope we don't lose that because I really think that is a #1 thing that's going to continue to make music pretty strong as we go," said James Weaver, Director of Performing Arts and Sports at the National Federation of State High School Associations.

Choral ensembles also responded to the challenges of the COVID-19 pandemic with a renewed focus on community. The choral arts rediscovered that while singing is what they do, at its heart is the sense of community that comes from a shared experience. Even though choirs could not make music (the very thing that brings them together), they still found a need to be together and were concerned about each other's well-being. Singers (amateur and professional) requested Zoom social meetings to maintain hope and relationships. Conductors reconceptualized the rehearsal to be more singer-focused by programming repertoire that was easier to connect to, producing part tracks to aid learning, and discussing its context. Organizations sought funding to pay performer contracts not because they had to but because they cared for their singers' well-being. All of these actions reflected a desire to maintain and strengthen the bonds of relationships, otherwise known as social capital,[2] a necessity in forging a sense of community in a group.

The choral community learned significant lessons during the COVID-19 pandemic that it would like to remember post-pandemic. While conductors may reflect on their individual programs, opportunities for reflection as an art form rarely occur. The pandemic pause disrupted the status quo in the choral community and provided a time for conductors to self-evaluate their program's priorities, strengths, and weaknesses. Directors and professional singers cited tools they would like to keep, such as their technological skills and the option of meetings on Zoom. In addition, some directors mentioned that with the murder of George Floyd during the pandemic, there was a double crisis. They realized they needed to create a more inclusive place of belonging in their rehearsals. As a result, they expanded their repertoire to include more pieces by those historically excluded, such as female-identifying and BIPOC composers. Directors also committed more time to unpacking the historical and cultural context of the pieces and situating them in today's world. They will continue using Zoom to bring culture bearers and BIPOC composers into their rehearsals. This lesson of inclusion is significant because if the choral art is a community in the truest sense of the word, it must be a place of belonging for all.

Change requires a disruption, and COVID-19 was a worldwide disruption to the choral art's status quo. If the thoughts of these choral leaders reflect the greater choral world, the choral art needs to reprioritize community, collaboration, and belonging—worthy words to describe this new era of singing. In going about creating and performing, the choral art may have lost some of these characteristics. The good news is that now is the opportunity for lasting changes to occur with structural changes in each area of the choral ecosystem. As seen in the NCCO, procedures were established so that lessons learned during the COVID-19 pandemic can live beyond the current leadership team. As Chorus America said, "Choral singing is a significant part of American life."[3] We should care for the choral art and its community if we believe that statement. If we do not, we risk losing a crucial element of our humanity and happiness.

It will take a long time for the choral world and the greater community to process the personal and societal toll of COVID-19. The opportunity for a paradigm shift is here—Can the choral art retain this renewed focus as a community of collaboration and inclusion? It can if it continues to remember that each breath and the opportunity to sing with one another is a gift. This collection of pandemic stories—of resurrecting song—is a part of that healing and growth process. May we honor the people and narratives to become a true community of song celebrates and champions all the stories yet to be told.

Notes

1. The Guardian, *Stayin' alive! How music has fought pandemics for 2,700 years*, https://www.theguardian.com/music/2020/apr/06/stayin-alive-how-music-fought-pandemics-2700-years-coronavirus
2. Moy, W. K. (2021). Come Together: An Ethnography of the Seattle Men's Chorus family. In R. Timmers, F. Bailes, & H. Daffern (Eds.), *Together in music: Coordination, expression, participation*. Oxford, UK: Oxford University Press.
3. Grunwald Associates LLC and Chorus America, *The Chorus Impact Study: Singing for a Lifetime*, https://chorusamerica.org/sites/default/files/resources/ChorusImpactStudy_SingingforaLifetime.pdf

Index

Note: Page numbers followed by "n" refer to notes.

Acapella app 36
access 29, 30, 42, 44, 59, 105, 126, 138, 142, 155, 157
Adam Show 6
Aeolians 57, 66
aerosol 24, 135, 136, 148–149, 150, 158, 160
aerosol-based disease transmission 148
African American Museum 126
An African American Requiem 98, 104
African Sanctus 8
American Choral Directors Association (ACDA) 58–59, 96–97, 127; commentaries in emails 151; community-building 153–154; conference 27, 57–59, 96, 127, 131–133, 136–139, 144–146, 155–157; contract of Dallas 147; Executive Committee 137; financial risks 139; leaders exchange 138; manual 137; National Board 138; Northwestern conference 27, 57, 145; protocols 137; Southern conference 132; Southwestern conference 146; virtual conference 136–137, 146; webinars and seminars 136; Western conference 145; working from home 136
American Guild of Musical Artists (AGMA) 93
American String Teachers Association (ASTA) 131
A New Harmony Workbook 158

Antigone 112–113
Apfelstadt, Hilary 130, 137–138, 151, 153–154, 156
Arirang 68
artistic directors 96
Atlantic Music Festival (AMF) 85, 86

Babb, Sandra 57, 58–59, 67, 71–72
Baldwin Wallace University 89
The Ballad of the Brown King 51
Barbershop Harmony Society: international competition 142; international convention 133; midwinter convention 133; resource guides 152; Zoom 142, 153
Bard Festival 95
Barnes, Jasmine 105, 106
Belle Voce 57
belonging 22, 101, 157, 161, 162
Benvenuto, Martín 120–121, 124–126, 129
Berkshire Choral Festival 17
Bernstein, Leonard 58
Beth, Liza 133
Big Sky 98, 108
BIPOC composers 16, 23
Black feminism 51
Black Lives Matter 44, 137
The Book with Seven Seals 5
Bradshaw, Steven 109
Brailey, Sarah 77, 79, 86, 88–90, 94–95
breath 20, 60, 92, 157, 162
Bridge Choral Collective 42

164 *Index*

Brooklyn Art Song Society 84
Burdick, Yvette Adam 4, 5–8, 18, 20, 24

The Cantata For A More Hopeful Tomorrow 15–16
Carols After a Plague 109
Carter, Nathan 126
Cause for Song 17
Centennial Elementary 7
Centers for Disease Control and Prevention 147, 150, 151
Cerrone, Christopher 110, 111
Chichester Psalms 58
children and youth choirs 2; affects of COVID-19 on programs 49–51; challenges 30–44; directors 26; keeping the hope alive 44–45; learnings 46–49; plans when COVID-19 emerged 27–30; positive moments 51–53; *see also* Choir School of Delaware; College Place Middle School; Edmonds-Woodway High School; Irwin Elementary School; Ledyard High School; Meadowdale High School; The Chorus of Westerly; Vancouver Youth Choir (VYC)
Choir School of Delaware: challenges 39–40; community partners 29–30; COVID-19 affects on programming 50–51; learnings during pandemic 47–48; positive moments from pandemic 53
Chor Amor 62–63
choral community 160; challenges 160, 161; disruption 161; learnings during pandemic 160, 161
choral organizations 130; challenges 135–151; learnings during pandemic 152–156; silver linings 156–158; *see also* American Choral Directors Association; Barbershop Harmony Society; Chorus America; National Association of Teachers of Singing; National Collegiate Choral Organization; GALA Choruses; National Federation of State High School Associations
Choral Public Domain Library (CPDL) 12
choral singing: Black feminism 51; feelings, choir members 1; rehearsals 10–11; *see also individual entries*
Chorus America 120, 162; federal emergency funding 141; PPP loan/grant 157; remote work 133; viral spread 140; virtual performances 141; webinar 140; workbook for choruses 157–158; Zoom socials 141
Chorus Impact Study (2019) 1, 2n1, 3
The Chorus of Westerly: challenges 4, 5–8, 40–42; COVID-19 affects on programming 20; emergence of COVID-19 pandemic 4; keeping the hope alive 18; learnings during pandemic 48; positive moments from pandemic 23–24
Chromebooks 32
Clueless 12
coalition 149, 158, 160
collaboration 29. 32, 70, 77, 130, 134, 158, 160, 161, 162
College Band Directors National Association 148
College Place Middle School: field trips 28; 35
collegiate choirs 152; affects of COVID-19 on programs 68–69; challenges 58–66; choral conductor 152; conductor-teacher 69; directors 55–56; keeping the hope alive 67–68; learnings 70–74; plans when COVID-19 emerged 56–58; positive moments 74–75; skills learned during pandemic 69–70; *see also* Cypress College; Hofstra University; Loyola Marymount University; McMaster University; Oregon State University; Oakwood University; Peabody

Index   165

Conservatory; Tarleton State University; University of Michigan; University of Nebraska-Omaha; Yale University
Colorado State University 135
Comcast 30
Cometa, Melanie 27, 45, 46–47, 49, 53
communication 7, 63, 102, 156, 158, 161
community 1–3, 5, 13, 17, 19, 20–24, 26, 29, 40, 44, 47, 52, 55–56, 59, 65, 67, 69, 72–74, 81, 98, 99, 106, 116, 118, 126, 130, 135, 136, 141, 142, 145, 153, 154, 160–162
community choirs 2; affects of COVID-19 on programs 16–20; challenges 5–18; and COVID-19 3; keeping the hope alive 18–19; learnings 21–23; plans when COVID-19 emerged 4–5; positive moments 23–24; *see also* Dallas Symphony Chorus; Mendelssohn Chorus of Philadelphia; One Voice Chorus of Charlotte; One Voice Mixed Chorus-Minneapolis; Skagit Valley Chorale; The Chorus of Westerly; The Washington Chorus; Trinity Lutheran Church of Worcester
composer 6, 12, 16, 22, 37, 48, 51, 68, 98, 106, 108, 109, 127, 129, 137, 160, 161
computational fluid dynamics (CFD) 150, 151
concerts 15, 22, 29, 33, 40, 52, 62, 67, 74, 77, 87, 95, 98, 99, 116, 128, 139, 154, 155, 157
connection 1, 3, 18, 20, 33, 40, 44, 47, 65, 99, 101, 105, 115
Considering Matthew Shepard 8
consistency 40
Conspirare 78, 85, 88, 97, 103
contract 77, 87, 93–95, 100, 107, 114, 115, 124, 143, 146, 161
Coronavirus Aid, Relief and Economic Security (CARES) 104

Country Music Association Foundation 70
COVID-19 pandemic 77; choral singing 1; collaboration 160; gigs 78; musical plans 77–79; music videos 81; new organization 120–123; online program 86; organization's plans 96–98; relief funds 9; singing, "high-risk" activity 1; singing through 94–95; soundtracks 82; spring 2021 85
creative 38, 80, 91, 102, 153
The Crossing 98, 106
Cypress College: positive moments from pandemic 74

Dallas Symphony Chorus: challenges 10; emergence of COVID-19 pandemic 5; learnings during pandemic 21
Davis, Cory 4, 12–13, 20, 21
Day, Andra 12
death 1, 3, 126
Dehoney, Catherine 24, 134, 135
Delta 144
DePreist, James 106
Dilworth, Rollo 40
DiOrio, Dominick 13–15, 19–20, 22–23
disease 147, 148, 160
diversity 68, 69, 99
Dona Nobis Pacem 9
Dorchester Canticles 58
Dower, Kellori R. 74
Down with the Rosemary and Bays 9
Duke Ellington School 17
Dunphy, Melissa 13–14

Easter Oratorio 84
Echoes 117
Edmonds-Woodway High School: Jazz Festival 28, 34–36
Ellis, Cindy 123
engagement 9, 16, 17, 22, 26, 65, 154
equity 22, 51, 104, 157
EXIGENCE 85, 96, 99

Facebook 56–57
Faruqi, Adam 77–78, 81, 88, 90, 94

166 Index

Ferdinand, Jason Max 57, 66, 70–71
Fetter and Air 13, 14
film studios 82
FitzGibbon, Katherine 96, 104, 115–117
Floyd, George 53, 98, 99, 137, 154, 158, 161
flu 155
The Forest 108
Fowler, Paul 117
Fox, Derrick 57–59, 67, 69–71
Fryling, David 69, 72
Fuller, Amy 131
funding 98, 104, 108, 110, 120, 128, 130, 139, 141, 149, 157, 160, 161

Galante, Brian 131
Gay and Lesbian Association (GALA) Choirs 106; Festival 2021 141; grant assistance 141; LGBTQ+ choral festival 134; queer community struggle 141
Geter, Damien 15, 98, 106
gigs 78
Google Classroom 30
Google Meets 32
Google Slide 30
Gordon, Michael 98
Gordon's Music Learning Theory 47
grief 77–95
guest 8, 17, 19, 40, 42, 58, 67, 126, 160

Habermann, Joshua 5, 10, 21
Hagenberg, Elaine 60
Hailstork, Adolphus 127
Halstead, Lucinda 135
Hamilton Children's Choir 65
Handel and Haydn Society 87
Harley-Emerson, Arreon 29–30, 39–40, 47–48, 50–53
Harper, T. J. 58–61, 67, 72, 75
Hawn, Crossley 77–79, 89, 91
health 17, 24, 53, 68, 100, 131, 136, 141, 154, 155
Henderson, Allen 139
Hilger, Robyn 130, 144, 152, 155
Hocus Pocus 13
Hofstra University: learnings during pandemic 72; new skills learned 69

Hogan, Moses 13
Hold On 13
Holiday 2020 concert 37
Holstead, Lucinda 140
Holy Trinity Bach Vespers 82
home 6, 22, 23, 27, 29–32, 36, 38, 39, 42, 43, 45, 49, 56, 57, 59, 66–68, 79, 80, 82, 84, 86, 87, 91, 100, 108, 111, 117, 125, 128, 133, 136, 154
Home and the Heartland 20
Home for the Holidays 100
hope 3–25, 35, 44, 67, 72, 84, 88, 89, 90, 114, 127, 141, 151, 152, 155, 158, 161
Horenstein, Jeff 27, 38–39, 44–45, 48–50
Howell, Andrew 4, 8–9, 18, 20, 23–24, 40–42, 48
Human Heart 127
humanity 160
Humming Chorus 10
Hyatt, Rob 28

Ich Habe Genug 79
I Love Being Here With You 49
iMovie 31–32, 67
inclusion 40, 162
inequity, 40, 105
infamous webinar 139
innovation 77–95
Inslee, Jay 28
isolation 61, 107, 108, 157
Irwin Elementary School: challenges 30–33; COVID-19 affects on programming 50; learnings during pandemic 47; positive moments from pandemic 51–52; student teacher 28

JackTrip 61
Jason Max Ferdinand Singers 120
Jaworski, Renee 111
Jazz Educators Network (JEN) conference 29
Jazz Festival 28
Johnson, Craig Hella 40, 96, 100–101, 115–117
Jones, David 92
Justice Symphony 15

Kallembach, James 112–113
Keep Our Voices Singing 99
A Killer Party 38
King 5 News 24
Kin to Sorrow 126
Kyr, Robert 97

Lancaster, Stephen 77–78, 84–85, 88, 91–92, 94
Lang, David 108, 109; *love fail* album 111
learning community 72
Ledyard High School: annual scholarship concert 27; challenges 36–38; COVID-19 affects on programming 49; financial grants 47; keeping the hope alive 45; positive moments from pandemic 53
Lee, Sunkyong, 68
Legacy Quartet Contest 142
Library of Congress 107
Lift Every Voice and Sing 99
livestreaming 8, 12, 18, 19, 29
lockdown 26, 42, 90, 144
Logic 116
Lorelei Ensemble 97, 110, 112
Los Angeles Master Chorale 78
Los Angeles Times 25n, 131, 159n
Loyola Marymount University: challenges 59–61; choir program plans 58; keeping the hope alive 67; learnings during pandemic 72; positive moments from pandemic 74–75
Lynch, Brian 130, 133–134, 141–142, 152–153, 157

Maroney, Kate 77–79, 82, 89, 92
Mass for Troubled Times 20
mask 7, 8, 14, 15, 38, 41, 56, 59, 66, 67, 71, 84, 85, 94, 99, 121, 123, 125, 131, 136, 144, 145, 146, 151, 155
McGill, Anthony 99
McGill, Stan 131, 138
McKinney, Christie 133
McMaster University: challenges 63–66; choir program plans 56–57; COVID-19 affects on programming 68–69; learnings during pandemic 73; new skills learned 69–70; positive moments from pandemic 74
Meadowdale High School Choirs: challenges 38–39; COVID-19 affects on programming 49–50; keeping the hope alive 44–45; learnings during pandemic 48–49; Northwest ACDA conference 27; positive moments from pandemic 51–52
Mello-Aires 34–36
Mendelssohn Chorus of Philadelphia: challenges 13–15; COVID-19 affects on programming 19–20; learnings during pandemic 22–23
mental health 17, 141
mentoring 40
Meyers, Jessica 113
Microsoft Sway 30
Miller, Shelly 148, 149
Miller, Jane Ramseyer 17, 22
Miller, Joe 15
mitigation 140, 150
Monson, Marty 134, 135
Moore, Michele 28, 30–33, 47, 50, 52
Morrow, David 144
Mozart Requiem 14–15
Mummert, Mark 4, 10–12, 19, 21–23
musical plans 77–79
music learning theory (MLT) 39, 47

Nally, Donald 96, 98, 106–107, 114, 117–118
National Association for Music Education 147
National Association for Music Merchants 147
National Association of Teachers of Singing (NATS) 87; collaborating webinars 134; programming with webinars 152; scientific studies 135–136; sharing ideas 135; summer national conference 134
National Endowment for the Arts 157
National Collegiate Choral Organization (NCCO): audio engineers 133; conductors

168 Index

133; governing philosophy 144; procedures 162; video conferencing 143; video engineers 133; webinars 133, 143
National Federation of State High School Associations: aerosolization activities 150; coalition of aerosol study groups 158; coalition of organizations 149; instrument cleaning 147; large-group contests 131; mitigation for masking 150; mitigation to reduce risk 150; state administrator meeting 156; working with manufacturers 147
National Shrine 79–80
National University of Costa Rica Choir 67
The Nearness of You 35
Nelson, Haydn 20
new choirs: auditioning singers 124; challenges 123–124; concept of 120; COVID-19 affects on programming 126–127; creativity 125; learnings during pandemic 128–129; performance 121; resilience 125; strength 125; *see also* Jason Max Ferdinand Singers; 21V
New York City 82
New York Times 137
North Seattle College 5
North Woods 113
NOTUS at Indiana University 22
Nova, Shara 110

Oakes, Vic 132
Oakwood University: challenges 66; choir program plans 57; learnings during pandemic 70–71
Obligations 117
Oh, Praise the Lord 127
Omicron 15, 85, 144
One Voice Chorus of Charlotte: challenges 12–13; COVID-19 affects on programming 20; emergence of COVID-19 pandemic 4; learnings during pandemic 21
One Voice Mixed Chorus-Minneapolis: financial grants 17; learnings during pandemic 22
online auditions 21, 73
online program 103
oral training skills 39
Ordway, Scott 113
O'Regan, Tarik 58
Oregon State University: challenges 58–59; keeping the hope alive 68; learnings during pandemic 71–72; Northwest ACDA conference 57
organizations 161; plans 96–98

Paulus, Stephen 126
Peabody Conservatory: learnings during pandemic 73–74; positive moments from pandemic 74
Performance Today 109
Performing Arts Alliance 139
Performing Arts Medicine Association (PAMA) 135
personal musicianship 71
Philadelphia Orchestra 15
plague 109
PPE (personal protective equipment) 113
Praise Song for Tulsa 121
professional choirs 96; challenges 99–114; COVID-19 affects on programming 117; EXIGENCE 99; funding challenges 108; learnings during pandemic 108, 115; mentor 103; online program 103; singing during pandemic 118; venue 104; Zoom 108, 115; *see also* Conspirare; The Crossing, EXIGENCE; Lorelei Ensemble; Resonance; Santa Fe Desert Chorale
Professional Choral Collective (PCC) 70
professional organization 104
professional singers 77–95; challenges 75, 79–87;

freelance 87; learnings during pandemic 90–94; musical plans 77; post-pandemic 90–94; pre-pandemic 92; protection for artists 93; protocols 95; singing during pandemic 94–95; teaching assistant 86, 88; unemployment 86; *see also* Sarah Brailey, Adam Faruqi, Crossley Hawn, Stephen Lancaster, Kate Mahoney
Pro Tools 116
protect yourself from infection 109

quarantine 38, 58, 79

Rachmaninov Vespers 100
racial reconciliation 99, 117
research 3, 61, 80, 106, 133, 136, 140, 148, 151, 160
Reese, Charlotte 28–29, 33–36, 46
record 9, 12, 14, 27, 29, 32, 34, 36, 41, 46, 61, 64, 72, 82, 83, 87, 98, 109, 112, 113, 116, 123, 147
Remembering: Singing Water 17
remote 39, 74, 133
repertoire 8, 19, 20, 26, 31, 40, 41, 42, 48, 50, 69, 112, 117, 122, 154, 161
Resonance Ensemble 96, 98
respiratory 5, 147, 148
resilience 39, 125
resurrecting song 130–158
ripple effects 139
Rise Up 12
Rising w/ The Crossing 107
risk 8, 95, 131, 139, 150, 162
Robertson, Troy 62–63, 73
Rogers, Eugene 5, 15–17, 23, 74
Route 66 49

Safe in His Arms 127
Santa Fe Desert Chorale 97, 99, 116–117
SATB choir 68
Schmidt, Franz 5
scientific community 136
self-producing organizations 113
Seraphic Fire 83

session choir 5
Seven Last Words of the Unarmed 57
Sharp, Tim 2, 17–18, 134, 135, 137, 138
Shaw, Caroline 20
sick 4, 15, 22, 60, 93, 123
Silent Night 100
Sing as One 12–13
Skagit Valley Chorale 3, 130, 131, 140, 149; challenges 4, 5–8; COVID-19 affects on programming 20; emergence of COVID-19 pandemic 4; keeping the hope alive 18; learnings during pandemic 24; livestream concert 8
A Slice of Pie 14
social capital 154, 161
social distancing 132
social justice 98
social emotional learning (SEL) 33
socio-emotional development 26
Songs of Unity 103
sophomores 35
sound engineer 83
soundtracks 82
Soundtrap 64, 65, 112; accounts 34
Spede, Mark 135, 147–149
Sphinx 99
Srebric, Jelena 149
St. Ignatius Loyola 82, 84
St. Matthew Passion 8, 19
Stockman, Tehya 150
Strength of Love 44
subscription series concert 40
superspreader activity 130
Swanson, Elizabeth 143

Tarleton State University: challenges 62–63; learnings during pandemic 73
technology 9, 32, 47, 56, 61, 80, 133, 136, 153, 156
Tennant, Carrie 29, 42–45, 48, 51, 52, 63
thematic programming 38–39
Thomas, Andre 40, 67, 137, 144, 155, 157
Threshold Choir 24
Time Capsule 43
To the Hands 20

Travel Guide to Nicaragua 98
Trinity Lutheran Church of Worchester: challenges 10–12; COVID-19 affects on programming 19; emergence of COVID-19 pandemic 4; keeping the hope alive 19; learnings during pandemic 21–22; positive moments from pandemic 23
Trumbore, Dale 22
Trump administration 1
Tulsa Chorale 17–18
Turandot 10
Twelfth Night 18
21V 120, 121, 125

Under the Overpass 105
University of Chicago 77, 87
University of Colorado 135
University of Michigan: COVID-19 pandemic impacts 74
University of Nebraska-Omaha: challenges 59; choir program plans 57–58; COVID-19 affects on programming 69; keeping the hope alive 67; learnings during pandemic 71; new skills learned 70
University of Notre Dame 77, 85
University of North Texas (UNT) 34, 35

vaccine 1, 88
vaccination 5, 7, 15, 145
Valverde, Mari Esabel 106
Vancouver Youth Choir (VYC): challenges 42–44; collaborations and arts organizations 29; COVID-19 affects on programming 51; keeping the hope alive 45; learnings during pandemic 48; positive moments from pandemic 51–52
Vasquez, Paul 123
Verdi Requiem 10
Virbela 142

virtual choir 6, 9, 12–13, 19, 21, 23–24, 31–32, 36–39, 49, 56, 58–60, 62, 67, 73, 82, 90–91, 94, 122, 154, 160
virtual concert 43–44
virtual parties 17
Voces8 series 66, 122
Vondrak, Kevin 108
VYC Kindred 51

Wachner, Julian 15
Warren, Scott 82
The Washington Chorus: challenges 15–17; emergence of COVID-19 pandemic 5; learnings during pandemic 23
Washington, Jamie 143
Washington Post 93
Wasileski, Hannah 110, 111
wave 84, 144
Weaver, James 130, 131, 135, 147, 156, 158, 161
We Hold Your Names Sacred 106
Weidenaar, Gary 132
We Shall Overcome 57, 66
Westerhaus, Tim 137
Westgate Elementary School 28
Westminster Choir College 50
WeVideo 9
Willer, Beth 73–74
Williams, Andrea 123
Wolfe, Julia 90, 97, 110, 112
Women's Suffrage 97
Wong, Tracy 56–57, 63–66, 68–70, 73, 74
World Health Organization (WHO) 1, 2n2, 148

Yale University: keeping the hope alive 67
You Can Plan on Me 109
You Do Not Walk Alone 60

Zielke, Steve 59
Zoom 5–8, 10, 16, 18, 22, 27, 29, 33–3, 42–43, 59–60, 63, 84, 85

For Product Safety Concerns and Information please contact our EU
representative GPSR@taylorandfrancis.com
Taylor & Francis Verlag GmbH, Kaufingerstraße 24, 80331 München, Germany

www.ingramcontent.com/pod-product-compliance
Lightning Source LLC
Chambersburg PA
CBHW052125300426
44116CB00010B/1786